HONESTLY
[REALLY LIVING WHAT WE SAY WE BELIEVE]

JOHNNIEMOORE

HARVEST HOUSE PUBLISHERS

EUGENE, OREGON

Cover by Koechel Peterson & Associates, Inc., Minneapolis, Minnesota

Backcover author photo by "DuckDuck Collective" www.duckduckcollective.com

Published in association with David Van Diest of D.C. Jacobson & Associates, 3689 Carman Drive, Suite 300, Lake Oswego, OR 97035.

HONESTLY
Copyright © 2011 by Johnnie Moore
Published by Harvest House Publishers
Eugene, Oregon 97402
www.harvesthousepublishers.com

Library of Congress Cataloging-in-Publication Data
    Moore, Johnnie, 1983-
    Honestly / Johnnie Moore.
       p. cm.
    ISBN 978-0-7369-3946-1 (pbk.)
    ISBN 978-0-7369-4114-3 (eBook)
    1. Christian life. I. Title.
    BV4501.3.M66465 2011
    248.4—dc22
                            2010050025

"Johnnie Moore's raw honesty will propel you to pursue an authentic walk with God."

"Most of us are looking for authenticity. We're turned off by people who talk big and don't deliver. That is especially true when it comes to the subject of religion. Johnnie Moore has given us an honest, believable book on what the Christian lifestyle is all about. I highly recommend it."

"*Honestly* is provocative and compelling—a godsend to a generation that is searching for truth. I hope everyone I know can read this book."

"I am breathing a huge sigh of relief for the next generation with leaders like Johnnie at the helm. This book will challenge all generations to get real in their walk with Christ."

"Johnnie Moore writes with a refreshing passion. His perspective on mission is first-rate, and his chapters on suffering and failure are reason alone to pick up this book."

"This is first-century Christianity in twenty-first-century narrative. Engaging. Interesting. Fun. Challenging. Biblical. This book gets it right!"

"Johnnie confronts issues we face head-on and brings them into focus with a kind of truth that is practical and dripping with compassion. *Honestly* is provocative, challenging, and healing."

"*Honestly* exhibits the earmarks of a revolutionary text...This book could well become a benchmark for our young adults."

GARY R. HABERMAS
distinguished research professor, Liberty University & Theological Seminary

"Johnnie Moore is a fresh voice of faith, bringing us a new message of challenge, vulnerability, and change."

ANGELA THOMAS
bestselling author and speaker

"This is must reading for those who want to take their faith seriously."

ED DOBSON
advisory editor, *Christianity Today*
author of *The Year of Living like Jesus*

"Johnnie Moore is essentially asking you to put up or shut up, get on board or get out of the way. When you're finished with this book, you're going to do one or the other."

JERRY B. JENKINS
novelist and biographer
owner, Christian Writers Guild and Jenkins Entertainment

"In this new book, Johnnie Moore shares his own journey to spiritual health through humorous and touching stories, and he challenges us to really live what we believe!"

WESS STAFFORD
president and CEO, Compassion International

"Johnnie Moore opens the wounds of his heart to show his journey to a true faith in Jesus...This book helps seekers believe in God and stand up for him in their daily lives."

RON LUCE
founder and president, Teen Mania Ministries

"Johnnie Moore writes with wisdom and insights far beyond his years. This new book gives all of us a lot to think about and put into action. Start reading and achieving."

PAT WILLIAMS
senior vice president, Orlando Magic
author of *Coach Wooden: The 7 Principles That Shaped His Life and Will Change Yours*

"Johnnie Moore encourages all followers of Christ to be real and to live with passion… His insights can help you take positive steps out of your own faith crisis."

JAMES ROBISON
president, LIFE Outreach International

"Johnnie Moore embodies the hope that American Christianity is not on its deathbed; rather, it's on the precipice of a new awakening. *Honestly* is definitely a must read!"

SAMUEL RODRIGUEZ
president, National Hispanic Christian Leadership Conference
Hispanic National Association of Evangelicals

"This book is a captivating look at faith and life. Johnnie Moore doesn't just write what he believes—he lives it."

VERNON BREWER
president, World Help

"This is an excellent book to read and then give to a friend who is on a quest for spiritual reality. And yes, doubts are welcome if they flow from an honest, searching heart."

ERWIN LUTZER
senior pastor, the Moody Church

"Johnnie Moore deeply loves God and wants us to experience something more than a surface relationship with him that has little impact on our daily lives…I'm so thankful he is guiding so many to experience what faith in God can really do."

PASTOR JIM CYMBALA
senior pastor, the Brooklyn Tabernacle

"Most Christians today haven't a clue about what they actually believe. This book is a wake-up call. If we're going to engage today's culture, our beliefs and actions have to match."

PHIL COOKE
filmmaker and author of *Jolt! Positioning Your Life for Lasting Change*

"*Honestly* is a refreshingly candid and deeply challenging charge to combat hypocrisy, monotony, and insignificance by embracing God's design."

MEREDITH ANDREWS
Word recording artist

"Johnnie speaks candidly about his own doubts and struggles with evil, suffering, and who God is, giving us permission to wrestle through our own doubts, peel back the layers of religion and hypocrisy, and discover a gut-honest and transformational relationship with Jesus Christ."

TIM CLINTON
president, American Association of Christian Counselors

"Johnnie Moore reminds a new generation that disappointment is inevitable and doubt is real—but disillusionment is optional."

DANIEL HENDERSON
founder and president, Strategic Renewal

"The journey from cynicism to sincere faith requires direction. Johnnie Moore leads you from a life of meaningless adherence to a vibrant relationship with Jesus."

ED STETZER
coauthor of *Transformational Church*

"Johnnie Moore is a phenomenal writer. This book is funny, sharp, and uplifting. I'm not part of the *We* in the subtitle, but I loved it anyway."

KEVIN ROOSE
author of *The Unlikely Disciple*

"Johnnie Moore paints a vision of what could happen if people in the global church actually chose to do what they say they believe. If applied, this book could change the world, literally."

JOHNNY HUNT
pastor, First Baptist Church, Woodstock, Georgia
former president, Southern Baptist Convention

"Johnnie Moore is a leader from within the millennial generation... I dare you to read his book with an open heart and a willing spirit. If you do, things will never be the same again."

RONNIE W. FLOYD
senior pastor, Cross Church, Northwest Arkansas

"Life is a grind. Each one of us has a story of conflict, pain, and hurt. There's no escaping it. *Honestly* does a fantastic job of linking our narrative of pain to our relationship with Jesus."

TED CUNNINGHAM
senior pastor, Woodland Hills Family Church, Branson, Missouri

"Reading this book is like looking into a mirror. Honest, reflective, and revealing. I've known Johnnie as a pastor, preacher, and missionary; now he is also one of my favorite new authors."

"This book is a treasure! Johnnie Moore brings an inspiring fresh perspective to freedom in Christ Jesus and soul care."

"Johnnie Moore writes with clarity and ease. His understanding of the human condition and what it takes to bring us into a genuine relationship with Christ makes this a groundbreaking book for those seeking to know Jesus as he deserves to be known."

"Johnnie Moore's strong rebuke of hypocrisy and his challenge to genuine Christianity will cause you to take an unsettling inward look at your own faith."

"I thank God for Johnnie Moore and for his deep concern for the salvation of the lost. May God use this book to stir hearts and minds toward that ultimate goal."

Andrea,

Truly, in the entire world,

there are too few words

to describe how deeply I love you.

You are my love, my joy, and my life.

I can't believe this is only the beginning!

Eu te amo, minha querida.

Acknowledgments

Writing a book is like getting a lot of loans. You pile up loads of borrowed advice and encouragement at nearly every intersection along your way. Unfortunately, I needed to ask more people than I can recall to help me along *my* way. All of those who read earlier versions of this manuscript or who deposited invaluable wisdom in my literary account are deserving of more gratitude than I can give. Truly, I couldn't have done this without them.

First and foremost, to my dear, adorable wife, Andrea, your constant support and encouragement, your wise insights, and your deep love pressed me on through the seasons of this journey. Thanks also to my mother-in-law, Eliana, and father-in-law, Rubens—your home provided a refuge for the development of these ideas. Thanks to my closest friends—Dad, Shawn and Cara George, Josh and Christy Straub, Clayton King, David McKinney, Chris Deitsch, and Michael Miller. Mentors like Ron Godwin, Don Fanning, Ben Gutierrez, Vernon Brewer, Luis Bush, Daniel Henderson, and the late Jerry Falwell are nearly solely responsible for anything of practical value I might add to this world. They have given me the gift of borrowed wisdom from their life experiences. I'm especially indebted to David Van Diest, John Van Diest, Don Jacobson, and Bob Hawkins. Of course, all the folks at Harvest House, especially LaRae Weikert, Terry Glaspey, and Gene Skinner have provided ceaseless encouragement and invaluable insight. I'm so grateful that you believe in me.

I also owe a great deal to several leaders and writers who gave me truly priceless advice and an accompanying gust of wind in my sails: Ed Hindson, Elmer Towns, Ron Hawkins, Tim Clinton, Luis Palau, Jim Cymbala, Wellington Boone, Lee Strobel, Calvin Miller, John Ortberg, Joni Erickson Tada, Erwin Lutzer, Gary Chapman, Mat Staver, Bob McEwen, Ron Luce, A.R. Bernard, Wayne Cordeiro, Ike Reighard, James MacDonald, Crawford Lorritts, Josh McDowell, Samuel Rodriguez, Miles McPherson, Leith Anderson, Ed Stetzer, Gary Haugen, Kenneth Copeland, Ted Cunningham, Gary Smalley, Dinesh D'Souza, Anne Graham Lotz, Don Marsh, Larry Crabb, Bruce Wilkinson, Karen Prior, Charles Billingsley, Jonathan Falwell, Tony Nolan, Thelma Wells, Dave Stone, Stu Weber, M.A. Thomas, Samuel Thomas, and David Nasser. I'm also grateful to my friend and the chancellor of Liberty University, Jerry Falwell Jr., for putting his blessing on this project and for leading our fantastic institution with such precision and vision.

Finally, to my mom, dad, and sister—thank you for allowing me to lay our wounds bare so that through them other wounded men and women will be healed. I love you all so much. And thank you to my friend and Savior, Jesus. I know this blessing came from you, and I want you to know that I'm so grateful that you have entrusted me with this opportunity. Truly, you work in strange and mysterious ways.

CONTENTS

Part 4: From Perseverance to Mission

Part 5: From Mission to Vision

FOREWORD
BY JONI EARECKSON TADA

Most people who will pick up this book are thirtysomething or younger. Perhaps the title caught your eye. It's a bit intriguing because, well…most people are *supposed* to live honestly, to live what they believe, especially if what they believe has anything to do with following Christ. But that's not always the case. Often a big gap develops between what people say they believe and what they actually do. And I'm guessing that's one dark road you don't want to go down. The last thing you want to be is a hypocrite.

Believe me, I understand. There was once a wide chasm between my words about Jesus and my walk with him. I wasn't fooling anyone, and deep down, I knew it. So right before heading to college, I realized I was going to have to make a decision. Would I truly live what I believed on campus, or would I believe something less? I didn't have to ponder the question long. Right before fall semester, I broke my neck in a diving accident. Suddenly, what I believed about God mattered in a huge way.

More than four decades have passed since that life-transforming accident, and how or to what extent God had his hand in it isn't so much the issue. The point is, I found God worth believing—and to believe him is to actually *live* him out in daily life. To do anything less is worse than unbelief.

People are looking for this today. Whether on a college campus, the office of a downtown financial center, or a home in a suburban cul-de-sac, young singles and couples are searching for more than what we baby boomers were able to hand off to them—especially as it concerns the Christian faith. The people who are currently filling university dorms, kick-starting their careers, raising new families, or serving abroad are tired of hypocrisy. They want the real thing. Authentic. Rigorous and robust. And worth following regardless of the cost.

The raw power of the gospel of Christ is inexorably drawing tens of thousands of young people into genuine kingdom living. And that's why so many in this restless generation are looking to Johnnie Moore for guidance. He's one of them. He's been there. And I've seen it firsthand. I was sitting in the Vines Center of Liberty University, preparing to speak to 10,000 students, when Johnnie, the campus pastor and vice president of Liberty University, stepped up to the podium. The place exploded. I could immediately tell this 27-year-old leader lived what he believed. His passion for his Savior and his love for his fellow students was unmistakable.

Johnnie Moore has a powerful word to impart to his generation. As he writes, "Spiritually healthy people live what they believe to be true. They are not hypocritical and halfhearted; they are not uncommitted and in perpetual limbo. They have settled on a few overarching truths that govern their lives, and they let those truths serve their role. They might still have questions and unresolved issues, but they are at least firmly planted on a few things, and those few things influence the way they think, live, and love the world around them."

And this is why you're holding *Honestly* in your hands. I pray that as you peel back the layers of what you believe, as you let Johnnie lead you deeper into the Scriptures, and as you seek the living God with a heart that's honest, you will discover that Jesus Christ *is* worth following on his own merits. May that timeless truth strike a match in your heart that will inflame a fresh passion to genuinely live what you believe and never turn back.

JONI EARECKSON TADA
Joni and Friends International Disability Center

INTRODUCTION

I was clammy, irritated, and in total misery. My temperature was 103 degrees, and I felt my body palpitating with every move of every limb. I was sick—very sick.

I wasn't exactly sure when I had contracted this virus during a 12-day excursion through northern India, but it was having its way with me. It hit me—as if I had run face-first into a brick wall—almost as soon as I climbed onto the airplane to come home, and it was clearly not planning on raising its white flag. The bug was engaged in a full-on air and ground assault against my system, and it was winning handily. I remember shaking violently in my townhouse with the heater cranked high enough to make a Bedouin sweat, amazed that something so infinitesimally small could nearly incapacitate a full-grown adult male. I had never been so sick, and I was shell-shocked and shivering.

Then my doctor said some awful words. "I think you have swine flu."

Swine flu! The global news media was in a panic as they depicted this mysterious scourge as a younger cousin of the Ebola virus that threatened to spark a worldwide pandemic. The media had been emphasizing four things that we had to fear in this changing world: nuclear weapons in the hands of rogue states, a global depression that could drain our money of its value, the most peculiar of pop-artists (Lady Gaga), and the assault of the swine flu from the coasts of Mexico to the ends of the earth.

Eventually my swine flu saga came to an abrupt conclusion because of one simple, game-changing experience. My doctor thumbed through his magic little book of medicine, stumbled upon the most commonly recommended remedy, and called a pharmacy. Within half a day I was aggressively engaged in my own assault against the little rascal that was making me miserable. It was on. Me against that little guy. Someone would win and someone would lose.

I won. Less than a week later, with a little bit of rest and the right prescription, I was good as new—healthy and strong and feeling victorious.

Diagnosis and Remedy

It's really quite amazing. An honest examination, the right diagnosis, and the right remedy can make a very sick person well again. That's all it takes. Identify the problem and prescribe the right solution. A good examination and the right medicine are the dual tools to make a sick person healthy.

This book is about becoming spiritually healthy by identifying and combating soul sicknesses that threaten to weaken our faith and inhibit it from producing the appropriate actions in our lives. Again and again, people tell me that their biggest struggle with Christianity is that Christians' beliefs and Christians' lives are incongruent. These folks say that Christians sound "high and mighty" or "holier than thou," but they don't love or live like Jesus did. In other words, they say that Christians are hypocrites.

Unfortunately, in many cases, I have to agree. For many of us in the church, our words and our actions don't always line up.

Hypocrisy is the swine flu that threatens the livelihood of our faith, and it can be caused by all kinds of things, such as doubt, an unbalanced spiritual diet, an improper perspective on life's problems, a lack of commitment to Jesus' mission, or a small vision of what God could do and wants to do through his followers. Those topics make up the five parts of this book.

We are all recovering hypocrites, but spiritually healthy people face this problem head-on. They are honest about their failures, so they repent and ask forgiveness instead of pretending everything is okay.

They are honest about their beliefs, so they embrace the truth and form strong convictions instead of bending to popular opinion. And they are honest about the implications of their faith—they know that believing Jesus is Lord means living out that confession in every aspect of their everyday lives.

Healthy Christians are not content to remain hypocritical and half-hearted; they are not uncommitted and in perpetual limbo. They have settled on a few overarching truths that govern their lives, and they let those truths serve their role. They might still have questions and unresolved issues, but they are firmly planted on at least a few things, and those few things influence the way they think, live, and love the world around them.

In some ways, this book is a soul checkup. It is written during a time when a lot of people seem to have a great affinity to faith of some kind but are simultaneously confused and bewildered by it. They are bewildered by public hypocrisy and confused because of their unanswered questions.

This is an honest book. In fact, at points, it might be a little too honest. It includes my experiences of fighting to find my own faith in the context of my parents' divorce and my ensuing and deeply painful journey from doubt to belief.

I don't want to preach at you through this journey. I won't be pointing any fingers or shouting any angry tirades. Rather, this book is a conversation over coffee between two well-intentioned but struggling friends. I want to talk to you as a friend—frankly, tenderly, and sometimes jarringly.

I don't intend to draw harsh and immovable lines in the sand. Instead, I want to open up a dialogue and have a chat as we take our time exploring together some important and personal parts of our lives. Let's honestly explore one simple question: What if we lived what we say we believe?

When all is said and done, I have a simple hope—that your soul will feel alive and that you and the world will be better for it.

PART 1

FROM DOUBT TO BELIEF

I f I do not believe, or if I struggle to believe, I am a doubter. In actuality, doubt has more to do with trust than with specific beliefs. The problem is not that doubters do not believe; they just do not trust. They might not trust God, his followers, or parts of his path.

A relationship with God, like all relationships, must begin with trust. This calls for more than answered questions. Trust is ultimately found in the courage to believe, and sometimes that courage is achieved only after a long season of struggle. The journey from doubt to belief can sometimes seem crippling, but in the end, it solidifies what otherwise could have been destroyed.

THERE HAS TO BE MORE TO THIS, RIGHT?
USING DISILLUSIONMENT TO LEAD YOU TO FAITH, NOT AWAY FROM IT

Everyone I talk to today seems to be disappointed with Christianity in some way. Well, guess what—so am I.

I hate admitting it, but if I'm going to be honest about my faith and my experience with Christianity, I have to come clean. I am ashamed of a lot of things.

Belief wasn't easy for me in the first place. It was an uphill battle for me to jump into a commitment to Christ and to settle a series of questions and challenges that warred against Jesus for my heart. And I'm a pastor, so if I feel this way, I can't begin to imagine what many others feel about faith in Christianity these days.

But I'm not just a pastor. I'm also a recovering doubter whose personal struggle to believe and to live those beliefs has been painful and difficult. On occasion, the struggle has been so difficult that I have been tempted to leave it all.

My Soul as Ground Zero

The war for my soul began sometime between middle and high school. My family was living in one of those Southern cities dripping with Christianity. Everyone in our city had life all figured out. To an almost ridiculous extent, our town resembled a sitcom from the 1950s. People dressed nicely, they lived in perfect little families in beautiful houses sometimes surrounded by white picket fences, and they were devout Christians who attended church every time the doors were open.

My family fit the mold. We went to church every Sunday, we lived a secure and affluent life, and most people thought we had it all figured out. This worked quite nicely because everyone we knew also seemed to have it all figured out. Everyone appeared to be sickeningly perfect.

The only problem was that my family didn't have it all figured out. We were actually more like a dramatic reality show than a 1950s sitcom. We were like *Jersey Shore* in Mayberry, and our situation was souring by the day. We attended church on Sunday, but we were bad Christians Monday through Saturday. We looked financially secure, but we were nursing enough debt to finance a space shuttle. We worked hard to look content with what we had, but we were never content with anything. Our perfect little family was actually a ticking bomb.

Looking like faithful Christians in the heart of the Bible Belt is easy, but the problem was that we never had a heart to our faith. We were like a body with arms and legs and hands and feet but no heart. What was most central was conspicuously absent.

We worked so hard to look good that somehow we neglected to actually live what we believed to be true. The Bible refers to this as having a form of godliness with no power. If we had honestly looked at ourselves, we would have noticed our glaring hypocrisy. Instead, we were self-deceived, oblivious to our hypocrisy or willfully ignoring it. Christianity was our culture, the core of our society. It was our social club and our clique. We went to church to see and to be seen by others. Our social circle was like any other—it just happened to be a religious one.

Oddly, we somehow didn't know all of this was wrong. Our lives were as broken as an arm with the bone protruding from the skin, but we just moved through the motions of life while totally ignoring our wound.

Living in such a spiritually anemic state and nursing this half-hearted kind of Christianity was so normal to us that we almost didn't know that a spiritually alive, committed faith even existed. Christianity was only our culture, not the subject of our devotion. It was like a fad with a long shelf life.

We weren't only fooling ourselves. Everyone else thought we were good Christians too. But we weren't.

Our Christian PR Stunt

I remember learning as a little kid how to put a smile on my face before walking through the church doors. My parents didn't teach me this directly. I sort of caught it, and if you grew up the same way I did, you probably caught it too.

Our routine became almost comical. Even if my family was engaged in all-out assault in the car on the way to church, we would smooth the wrinkles out of our Sunday best, plaster fake smiles on our faces, and get ourselves together before walking into the sanctuary like politicians waving at the crowd. Every time someone asked us how we were doing, we would say, "Fantastic—life is good!" We were robotic and plastic and bogus despite our best intentions. In hindsight, the whole scenario is absurd, but it was our reality, and we were oblivious to the way we were inadvertently but tragically destroying our family.

Our Christianity was actually one big PR stunt that we had carefully crafted in order to look good. Our phony and frantic smiles hid the truth: My churchgoing parents' marriage was on a respirator, and our family life was spiraling out of control. We were hemorrhaging. Our crash was imminent.

Behind our carefully manicured exterior was the slow and tedious *tick...tick...tick...* of a bomb about to explode. Either people didn't hear it or they chose not to do anything about it. No firemen or caring neighbors came to rescue us. Our fate was sealed, even in the presence of the only people who could save us, in the only place that could bring us restoration. Maybe our potential rescuers were too busy nursing their own PR stunts.

Hurting people or families who die in a church are like sick or injured people who die in a hospital. You can die in a hospital in one of two ways. You can die on the operating table, or you can die in the waiting room. We never made it to the operating room, and no one in the waiting room noticed that things were so bad because we hid our problems so carefully.

Actually, we were gushing blood on the inside.

Out of Desperation

When my parents finally saw what was really happening in our family, it was almost too late. For a while they had known that something was badly broken, but pride and an obsession with peoples' opinions kept them from getting the help they needed.

Things finally became bad enough that my parents gathered the courage to ask for help. They only did it once. They knew things were already critical and that the prognosis was dire. They knew they couldn't ignore or hide their problems any longer, and they really didn't want their relationship to die. They knew this probably meant they would become the talk of the town, but the time had come to call 911. It was time to exercise their last-ditch effort before the bomb exploded.

So they took a deep breath, picked up the phone, and scheduled an appointment with a pastor at our church. They hoped that a man of God, led by the Spirit of God, would be able to bring healing into their impossible situation. This appointment was an act of desperation. They knew the damage was nearly irreparable.

They opened their hearts to that pastor with buckets of painful tears. They pleaded, "What can you do to help us? We will do whatever we have to. We just need help."

That's when the bomb exploded. Their last-ditch effort failed. The heart of their relationship flatlined, and everything went spinning wildly out of control.

Within months my parents were divorced, and our affluent family was living in minor-league poverty. Our bank foreclosed our mortgage and repossessed our cars, my mom was drowning as she tried to hold her life together, and my dad was sinking deeper and deeper into despair. Eventually, he narrowly survived his first suicide attempt—in my presence.

Why I Am Jaded

Sometimes pastors try really hard to help people. They are well meaning and well equipped to address people's problems, and they deposit all the advice they can into the lives of those who seek them out. But ultimately, the people they are counseling must decide whether they want to change and be healed. If the people refuse to accept or apply the counselor's wisdom and they continue to struggle, that's their fault, not the pastor's fault. The people have to take the medication the pastor prescribes, or they will remain sick and could eventually die. A pastor fulfills his responsibility by making wisdom available and by trying to motivate them to use it. If they choose not to apply it, they have blown it. The counselor is an advisor, not a wizard.

But occasionally, pastors blow it too. That's what happened with the pastor counseling my parents, and the collateral damage almost cost me my faith.

Et Tu, Brute?

I can't quite remember when I learned that the pastor counseling my parents was also having an affair with another pastor's wife. But I remember my reaction. I almost had to go to the emergency room. My heart seemed to stop beating for a few seconds. I felt betrayed. I was suddenly Julius Caesar lying in a pool of my own blood from a wound inflicted by Brutus and Cassius, compatriots turned traitors.

I began to wonder if my parents might have been healed had their pastor-counselor been as excited about his relationship with God as he was about his undercover relationship with another man's wife.

Unfortunately, he wasn't attuned to the Holy Spirit. He was attuned to lust, and as a result, he willingly committed malpractice. My mom and dad had inadvertently visited a washed-out surgeon for a critical procedure. This surgeon knowingly worked on them with an expired license, and my family was a casualty.

That pastor needed God's wisdom because my family was in real trouble. They were in the kind of trouble that required supernatural intervention. They needed a helper who was plugged into a miracle-working God, a God who had appeared in fiery furnaces, who had brought life from death, and who loves to reconcile broken lives.

My parents were probably just another appointment in that pastor's day. Another name on his full calendar, another couple he could dole out some advice to. He sat in front of my broken parents and told them how to heal their relationship at the very moment that he was sabotaging two. Somehow, this man who was responsible for helping heal relationships had become a killer of relationships—in God's name.

I'm sure the guy gave some good advice, but his advice could not have been seasoned with the anointing and power of God. He had let his license lapse.

Getting over the scars from this situation has taken me a long time. I know much more about the grace of God today than I did then, and I've learned to view that pastor through God's eyes, but I still would have a really hard time looking him in the eye. I'm still nursing the wounds he helped carve into my tender, young heart.

Have you ever felt this way?

Hypocrisy Hurts

Nothing is worse than being totally disappointed by someone you should have been able to totally trust, right? Your heart shatters like a glass that falls from the top shelf. Even if you could put that shattered glass back together, it would still bear the crooked scars of its traumatic fall. Public hypocrisy leaves scars.

I meet a lot of people who have been deeply hurt by Christians. These people are tending to wounds inflicted by supposedly trustworthy people. In some ways, these are the worst kind of wounds. The victims feel betrayed, disappointed, disillusioned, and just plain hurt.

The situation worsens when seemingly every other month a new story comes out about the public failure of a prominent Christian. You've probably heard so many stories of preachers' scandals, you could almost predict the next one. If you're like me, every time you hear of another religious scandal, you almost feel sick. Your stomach drops to your toes the way it did when you rode a too-big roller coaster. After the initial shock, your stomach churns cartwheels against gravity. Sick.

That's how I feel when I hear another story like my story. I get woozy. I'm angry and sad simultaneously. I stare at the news for what seems like a week, and then my head shakes in disbelief as it falls into my hands. "Say it isn't so." Public failures fall like bombs into the body of Christ. When they hit, some people's faith dies on impact. Other people are injured and nurse the scars for years.

I didn't die when I was at ground zero, but I was jarred pretty badly, and in some ways I'm still scarred. Thankfully, I'm recovering, but sometimes people don't recover. Personal experience with hypocrisy can be that traumatic.

I know that not all pastors are major-league hypocrites, but every outlandish example of public failure triggers an earthquake in my soul. It shakes me. I feel it in my bones, and I wonder if anyone will trust *me* anymore. After all, I am a rookie pastor myself.

My Faith Is Jaded, but It's Not Dead

This whole experience caused me to doubt my faith, and this book is largely a story of my fight to preserve and to live my belief despite my personal weaknesses and disappointment with certain characteristics of popular Christianity.

I now know that my parents' divorce and that pastor's hypocrisy collided in my faith experience and that the wreckage included a sense of disillusionment with many Christians and many churches. I must confess—I've become a bit jaded. I think a lot of Christians are jaded, especially Christians who've grown up in largely Christian nations like the United States.

So I'll just come clean from the beginning. "My name is Johnnie Moore, and I am a pastor, but I'm nursing some serious trust issues with Christianity."

Ooh, that feels better. You should try it.

Please don't misunderstand me—my issue isn't with Jesus, but with his followers. I love God with all my heart. I believe Jesus rose from the dead, I believe that the Bible is God's Word and that the Holy Spirit is our counselor. I really want to be devout, and I really want to live an honest faith. I want to actually live what I say I believe. But stereotypical Christianity just wears me out. I get tired of insulated pastors with plastic smiles who preach about life but know nothing of the reality a lot of us are facing. I hate cheap, haphazard answers to really hard and important questions. I can't listen when people speak authoritatively about problems they clearly know nothing about.

I believe Christianity has more to offer than what a lot of us have witnessed or experienced. It is more than we have seen and heard, more than the faith of hypocrites and casual, barely committed "believers." Faith doesn't have to be one big PR stunt. Somewhere a secret garden holds a buried treasure, a hidden truth, a Pandora's box of belief, and when that box is opened, joy and a living, supernatural faith flow out.

This book asks what happened to the kind of Christianity that caused men to choose martyrdom before denying Jesus or that was marked by miracles and real change in really unlikely lives. Why do we so rarely see angry men like Saul turn into servants like Paul if our culture is so saturated in Christianity? What happened to the power of the gospel? And what could happen if our beliefs made it into our daily lives?

I believe that true Christianity *is* powerful, it is not laced with hypocrisy, and it is alive. It is stunning, expansive, relevant, and life changing. It's not fake, like the whitewashed tombs that Jesus spoke of, and it's real.

I believe that when Jesus, the death defeater, really lives in our lives, *this* is what our faith will be. It will look like God is involved in my life and not simply that I'm hanging out with a bunch of people I barely like.

Over the past few years, I've searched for answers to the questions that sparked my disillusionment. I've discovered a lot of my own spiritual weaknesses, and I've learned that being jaded or being a bit frustrated with organized religion isn't all bad. A fight for belief can be destructive, but it can also bring life and conviction.

I decided to turn my frustration with some Christians and their churches into a search for authentic faith. The good news is that I think I've found it. I've discovered a kind of faith where we can explore our issues. It's the kind of faith that talks openly about struggles instead of burying them under a pile of Christian makeup. It's the kind of faith that isn't measured by how many church services you attend or how many verses you can recite or how many notches you've accumulated on your belt. It's the kind of faith that strikes a chord of love and affection in your heart. It's a faith so peculiar that a rich man would sell all to gain it. It causes people to exchange their bandages for real healing.

This faith turns new pages in history and releases the miraculous now, today, in the lives of regular people. This faith woos you into a deeply loving relationship with God.

Authentic faith can come from a season of doubt and searching and questioning that ultimately leads to a commitment. This search produces a refined faith that eventually empowers you to honestly and even recklessly live what you believe.

Your search may seem perilous. It might begin from a jaded place, but it can actually guide you to deeper faith and not away from faith.

As for me, my search gave me a passion for the deep, true, and living faith that I read about in the Bible, that I heard about in the stories of church history, and that I witnessed in some places in the world where becoming a Christian requires great personal sacrifice.

When I think about all of this, a simple question comes to my mind: What if?

What if we decided that to the best of our ability, we would no longer live a hypocritical, halfhearted Christianity that results in unbelief and disappointment? What if we decided to not be lukewarm? What if we took all the energy we spend in doubt and frustration and used it to trust and believe? What if we went on a pursuit to actually answer our nagging questions instead of using them as excuses to avoid commitment? What if we chose to run toward God even when our disappointment with hypocrisy threatens to chase us away from him? What if we decided to actually live what we believe to the extent that people's destinies are changed and Christ is more famous because of Christians and not in spite of them?

A Polite Request

In the end, I found something worth telling you about. It's real, it's authentic, and it's powerful.

For you, I have a simple question. I know you might have every reason in the world to doubt Christianity or to be angry with Jesus' followers. I know you might be spiritually weary or frustrated or tired. I know you might be on the verge of just settling for a cultural monogram of Christianity, or you may even be on the verge of leaving it all.

Still, I just have to ask—regardless of where you are in your faith journey, would you choose to follow me through this book with a spirit to grow, to learn, and to change?

Will you go with me?

I know it's a big question for a stranger to ask. It's probably hard for you to trust me with such a deeply important and carefully guarded part of your life. You don't know me well, and you're probably a little disappointed with some Christian leaders.

The reputation of some Christians has left a lot of mistrust on the table. That might make it hard for you to let down your guard and engage your heart in this journey. But I want to politely ask you to open your heart. Do this for the sake of your soul and for the chance that there is more to all of this than you realize. And up front, I have one commitment to make to you as we embark on this journey. I will be honest with you.

I'll be honest about my own struggles and my own questions. I'll unveil some of my own carefully guarded doubts, and I will not hold back when I feel like we've missed something critical.

Let's get somewhere together.

PROUDLY DOUBTING THOMAS
WHY THOMAS SHOULD BE CELEBRATED

[2]

My parents' divorce wasn't easy for any of us. My mom and dad suddenly became archenemies. Superman and Lois Lane turned into Batman and the Joker.

Despite their best and sometimes inadvertent efforts to pit me against each other, I learned that there is rarely a good guy and a bad guy in divorce. Divorce brings out the worst in people, and almost always both parties bear some responsibility for it. There are no winners and losers; there are only losers when a family is broken.

You've probably seen all of this unfold before. After a slow escalation of conflict, eventually the lid blows off, the two warring parties hop into survival mode, and from some primitive place in their psyche, they decide to pull out their weapons and fight.

When you're in middle school, being in the middle of a divorce is a lot like standing unarmed in the middle of a gunfight. You dodge the crossfire, and when it's all over, the gunfighters probably aren't the only ones with wounds. Most of the time, you leave the fight pretty banged up yourself.

Every passing conversation between my parents ended up atomic. They would step out of character, don again their war clothes, and stagger back into battle. My inoffensive mom ripped the phone off the wall and hurled it across the room. My businessman father became uncontrollably angry and often said hurtful things for the sole purpose of

31

wounding the woman he actually still loved. Mom and Dad weren't even able to decide where my sister and I would meet my dad for a weekend. Within a split second the whole conversation would melt down. Weapons would be drawn, and there we'd be again, dodging crossfire.

Every discussion was as tenuous as a peace negotiation between the Israelis and the Palestinians, and every attempt to make a simple decision resulted in chaos and carnage. I don't think Mom and Dad ever actually wanted to kill each other, but sometimes they acted as if they did. And as in all wars, there was collateral damage.

The whole situation was like a rack—the medieval torture device that pulls limbs from bodies with the turn of a crank. Every fight between my parents was another turn on the crank, pulling me apart between two people I loved deeply.

My sister and I became increasingly insecure about life as we watched our normally meek and benevolent mom and our incredibly generous and faithful dad locked in a battle that ripped the life out of their formerly loving relationship.

Today, my mom and dad are both in wonderful new relationships, but they speak of their divorce season the way war vets talk about Vietnam or the Persian Gulf. They have battle scars and lingering pain. If you've been close to divorce, you probably know this pain. A lot of divorcees live the rest of their life in bandages.

Enter Doubt

When the bombs were falling and the bullets were flying in my home, I started questioning the goodness of God. I found myself looking perplexingly at the sky and wondering where God was when my family was fracturing. Was he sleeping? Was he ignoring us? Was he up to more important things?

Soon my once stalwart, childlike faith was in dire shape as I asked myself very difficult questions about God's existence and about Christianity. I slowly wandered down the path of my personal pain and found myself doubting God increasingly. I felt that my doubts were totally justified given my circumstances. God had questions to answer, and I wasn't going to let him off the hook!

But the more I danced with doubt and the more I blamed God, the more terrible I felt about myself. I just couldn't believe I had the gall to doubt him, but somehow I did anyway. In hindsight, the whole scenario was so confusing. I didn't necessarily choose to doubt; the doubts just showed up in my mind one day. They were unwelcome guests, but they had arrived whether I wanted them there or not.

This presented a huge problem because my culture didn't allow people to doubt or question God. God wasn't to be doubted; he was to be obeyed, and doubters were judged and criticized. They were not helped. They might as well have been adorned with a big scarlet *D* so they could be avoided as if they were contagious.

So there I was in a faith crisis with no one to turn to who wouldn't judge me.

I was afraid to search for the answers I desperately needed because I thought Christians would think horribly of me. After all, I had been raised to maintain that manicured exterior when it came to my faith. Breaching that exterior was not an option.

I was encountering my first spiritual storm. It was vicious and relentless, and there were no coast guard skimmers in sight. My anchor was broken, and I was adrift in a sea of questions.

Doubting Thomas

I now know that seasons of doubt are perfectly natural when life gets a little bumpy, but I didn't know that then.

As if the war between my parents weren't difficult enough, I waged another war in my heart. On one hand, I knew I needed God, but on the other hand, I was deeply perplexed by him. I was questioning and doubting him, but oddly enough, I was still beating down his door, begging him to pay attention to me.

I was confused by everything going on around me, but still I went to sleep crying out my prayers to God. The whole situation was spiritually disorientating. I was caught in a quagmire of unbelief, and I didn't want to be in the quicksand. I didn't ask to be there, and I didn't jump into it. Yet I was there, and I knew that if I didn't fight my way out, I would sink.

I felt like the world's most famous doubter, the apostle Thomas.

I wanted so much to believe that Jesus was alive, and everyone had told me that Jesus was alive, but I just needed something more. I needed to experience Jesus' new life in *my* life. I needed to know he was up to something in all of this insanity and that he wasn't indefinitely leaving me to fend for myself. I wanted and needed to believe that God had my situation under control, but convincing myself of that was becoming increasingly difficult. I felt as if my faith had been submerged under an enormous tidal wave of disbelief. It was tossing and turning me violently in its wake. I was gasping for air with salt water in my nose, and sometimes I thought I was going to drown.

I remember sitting in church as a child listening to a teacher talk about the apostle Thomas. She didn't like him. Her tame Bible lesson took a nasty turn when it was time to talk about Doubting Thomas. Her face contorted into a judgmental snarl.

"Okay, boys and girls, we're going to talk about Thomas today."

Her nose crinkled as if she had smelled rotten food. Maybe she was foaming at the mouth…I don't remember. But I do remember that she liked Thomas about as much as I liked eating a cute little goat in India (more about that later).

For her, Thomas was a bad kid for one simple reason: He doubted God. He refused to take the other disciples at their word, and he insisted on touching Jesus himself. Thomas was, therefore, an embarrassment to Christianity.

The teacher stuck out her little crooked finger. It was horrifying. She barked, "Boys and girls, never be like Thomas. Never doubt God!" I left that lesson scared of doubting.

I wasn't actually afraid of God. I was afraid of the snarling teacher who I think should have had a name like Cruella. I was sure she would find out if I ever doubted God, and then she would track me down or rise from the dead and beat me senseless with her gigantic Bible. In the South, some Sunday school teachers are *tough,* and Cruella was the mother hen.

But do you remember the actual story of Thomas? Like many great stories, it begins with tragedy. Jesus had died, and the disciples scattered in disbelief.

Jesus' death left a lot of people disappointed and confused. They had watched him perform miracles and had heard him proclaim his deity. They had listened to his teachings, and many people thought he would eventually unseat Caesar and establish God's kingdom on earth. After all, he did say he was the Son of God, the Messiah, and he had walked on enough water to convince people of it. Yet for some reason, he had been unable to stop his own murder.

Some of the disciples thought his death had brought the end of their adventure, and a lot of them immediately initiated their backup plans. Matthew might have considered going back to tax collecting, and Peter might have been able to untangle his nets.

Imagine how the disciples felt watching the Son of God and King of kings totally defenseless in the hands of the Romans. Even Peter ("the rock") buckled when inquisitive passersby asked him about his connection with Jesus. With hardly any prompting, Peter denied his friendship with Christ three times.

After watching Jesus die in a bloody mess, nearly all of his followers scattered like flies. They were fair-weather friends who didn't want their own crowns of thorns. I bet some of them had nightmares for days, and no one could believe what had happened. One thing was sure. The Romans and Jews alike thought that Jesus' death signaled the death of his movement.

Then, you might remember, everything changed. In a roller-coaster tale, faith eventually unseats disbelief, and Jesus stands triumphant. The tomb was empty, and dozens of Christ's followers had seen him. The adventure that had appeared to be dying was clearly only beginning.

The disciples had needed a miracle. Now they had their miracle, and they had an empty tomb to prove it. They immediately convened a meeting in an upper room to regroup, and everything was moving along nicely for everyone—except Thomas.

The other apostles, even the eyewitnesses, had spent hours trying to persuade him. They went on and on about seeing the Lord personally. Some of them described running into Jesus on the road to the village of Emmaus, others had seen the crazy cocoon of burial clothes he had left behind, and everyone was mesmerized by Jesus' ability to manhandle the two-ton stone that guarded his tomb. Numerous people gave eye-witness accounts of Jesus' appearances.

Thomas was like a rock in his skepticism. The doubter would not believe. The others' testimonies had little effect on Thomas. They just weren't convincing because the stories were *their* stories. Thomas knew he couldn't make himself believe without his own experience. He had to see Jesus, to touch him, and to know he could trust him again. He wasn't content with a secondhand faith.

Eventually Thomas had enough of their persuasive efforts. He barked in frustration, "Unless I see the nail marks in his hands and put my finger where the nails were, and put my hand into his side, I will not believe it."[1] The jury was still out for Thomas.

Jesus must have heard Thomas' little rant because he showed up in the upper room, and he invited Thomas to slide his fingers into his scars.

This experience with Jesus became Thomas' first step into radical belief.

Rethinking Thomas: Doubter or Searcher?

I was raised to think of Thomas as an embarrassment to Christianity, but I now see him differently. I don't judge him anymore. In fact, I would rather spend time with Thomas than with Cruella. Somehow I find solace in Thomas' frustration with Jesus. Thomas was unwilling to settle for anything less than firsthand faith.

Thomas didn't care much to hear about the resurrection of Christ from others. He wasn't going to settle for their testimonies. He wanted his own testimony. He wanted to be an eyewitness himself. He is primarily known as a doubter, but I think there's more to the story. He was a man on a search for true faith. He was looking for the kind of faith I was writing about earlier. Thomas wanted to know for himself what everyone else had told him was true. He wanted good reasons to believe before he recommitted his life to a cause that might cost him his life. He wanted to stand on his own two feet or not stand at all, and he had decided he would not live perpetually on the shoulders of other people's faith. He would own his belief, or he would not believe. He needed firsthand reasons to believe.

Because of all of this, I don't believe Thomas is an embarrassment to Christianity. He is actually one of our prizes. He's like Paul and Peter, Moses and Noah, Abraham and David. He is a prize because Jesus revealed himself to him, and his search for faith led him into such radical commitment that he eventually became a martyr.[2]

All of this happened because something in Thomas' psyche ran deeper than his doubt. His doubt first came from a desire to know truth. Thomas was not trying to run from the truth. He simply wanted his own Jesus experience.

In fact, Thomas' doubt was actually a catalyst for a pure search for something more and something deeper. His doubt came from his desire to know Jesus for himself for sure, not from a desire to leave Jesus in disbelief. In fact, I don't think Thomas wanted to leave his faith at all. I think he was a tenderhearted man who was protecting his heart from being broken again. He knew he couldn't participate in this saga any longer unless Jesus really was alive.

He was trying desperately to hold on to his faith despite the crisis of Jesus' crucifixion. This is most apparent by the fact that he was with the other apostles in the upper room. He wasn't faithless. He had enough faith to be there. Deep inside Thomas' heart, he really did believe, but he also suspected that Jesus, his friend, had an experience just for him.

Meanwhile, Jesus knew what Thomas needed to believe, and Jesus was willing to give it to him.

Actually, I know many Christians who would benefit from being more like Thomas. They need to engage in their own search for truth and not be like so many Christians who live their entire lives through the faith experiences of other people without ever owning their belief for themselves.

Christianity is filled with believers whose commitment to Christ is purely cultural or familial. Their belief is not necessarily their conviction. It's their parents' or pastor's or culture's conviction. Their culture or their family drew them to church, to do good things, to go to a Christian college, or to identify themselves as Christian.

Way back in cultural Christians' family history, some broken man or woman or child fell on his or her face at the altar of a church, begging for the mercy of God, and to this day the succeeding generations have identified themselves as Christians. The only problem is that these descendants haven't had their own moments of falling on their faces at the altar, begging for the mercy of God. They are Christian because Grandma or Grandpa was Christian, and that's their foundation of belief.

This is why we actually need more men and women like Thomas in the church. We need men and women who aren't content to live out their beliefs on the fumes of other people's relationship with God. We need people who own their own faith and whose trust in God is based on their own conviction.

Thomas Seasons

When I first started feeling an affinity with Thomas, I was embarrassed. I guarded my secret doubts as if I were engaged in some kind of espionage. Now, my perspective is drastically different. I wear my Thomas season like a crown.

I needed to have my own Jesus experience for my faith to survive. Clearly, my mom and dad's faith wasn't sufficient to keep their marriage together. The faith of their counseling pastor wasn't sufficient to keep him from a life of hypocrisy, and the faith of many of the church-attending people I knew didn't seem to practically affect the way they lived their lives.

I now realize that many of my doubts came from my own desperate search to know for myself what I believed to be true. I was like Thomas, whose complicated search for the truth has too often and too easily been deconstructed into coldhearted doubt. In the end, my Thomas season didn't send me away from Christianity; it helped me to dig my footings for future faith. It helped me go deep in a world of wide but shallow belief. It helped me at last to honestly live what I believed to be true, and I found the justification I needed to choose to trust instead of doubt.

The doubt that was sparked by my family's drama ended up becoming the key to the solidification of my belief. It became the catalyst that caused me to live what I believe, and it launched me on a search to distinguish the authentic from the counterfeit in my faith life.

I began to dig through the Bible and read about followers of Jesus who were radically committed. These stories were in stark contrast with many of the lukewarm and half-baked Christians I knew. Christians in the Bible were willing to live extreme lives for God! They gave away large portions of their possessions for the good of the poor, they had the courage to stare down lions in coliseums, and they were willing to walk barefoot down burglar-infested roads to tell others about Jesus. The Bible refers to the early Christians as peculiar, and it says that Christians were in the world but not of it. There was something otherworldly about the people who first followed Jesus, and something about their faith journey was drastically different from many of ours today.

My Thomas-like search for belief led me to ask what biblical Christians knew about Jesus that I don't know, and what about their faith journey was different from my own. Honestly, I had good reason to be a little jaded with Christianity and to be skeptical of other believers' experience, but rather than packing my bags, I somehow determined that I needed to seek out Jesus for myself. I found that he is better and more glorious than even the best secondhand stories.

Some people do run away from God when they enter into seasons of doubt. They run as far away as fast as they can, and they transfer all of their frustration and bitterness and anger with life onto God. For some reason, I wasn't able to actually run away. Believe me, I tried. Ultimately, I couldn't leave without engaging in my own search for truth.

Touching Jesus

When life gets ferocious, many Christians wonder and doubt, but few admit it. There are more Thomases among us than we would ever expect. Unfortunately, the church is not often a safe place for people to admit and explore their secret questions.

At first, we think these seasons of spiritual crisis are dangerous, and sometimes they are. But oftentimes these seasons become catalysts for deeper, more authentic faith. Our seasons of doubt might not be the end of our faith, but the beginning of it.

This was Thomas' experience. Jesus didn't hold Thomas' doubt against him. Instead, he invited Thomas to touch his wounds. He knew what Thomas needed to believe. So Jesus gave it to him, and he did it because he loved Thomas. The apostle who some might have deemed the weakest believer in the bunch turned out to be one of the few who actually was able to touch the salvation-birthing wounds of Christ. Thomas dared to question for his own soul's sake, and God was gracious enough to give him the answers and the evidence he needed.

Thomas' season of doubt didn't become a life of doubt. Eventually, according to church tradition, Thomas traveled to the southern part of India as a missionary. He died there as a martyr. Today, Thomas' church still lives in India. A 2000-year-old Christian tradition continues to survive in one of the least Christian of nations because of the "doubting apostle."

Thomas' doubt was eventually exchanged for a radical commitment to live for Christ.

I can imagine him on the southern tip of India, testifying to followers of Hinduism about the day he touched Jesus' wounds. Maybe he finished his sermon by saying, "By his wounds I was healed." By the time Thomas reached India, he believed enough to die for what he believed. Searching Thomas had found something worth his life and death.

THE LIBERATION OF BELIEF
WHY BELIEF IN GOD MAKES SENSE

3

Elie Wiesel was 15 years old when he and his family were captured in their Transylvanian home and transferred to Hitler's largest concentration camp. Wiesel speaks of the images branded on his psyche in his book *Night*.

> Never will I forget that night, the first night in the camp, which has turned my life into one long night, seven times cursed and seven times sealed. Never shall I forget that smoke. Never shall I forget the little faces of the children whose bodies I saw turned into wreaths of smoke beneath a silent blue sky.

In Auschwitz, Wiesel lost his mother and younger sister before he and his father were transferred to Hitler's second-most infamous concentration camp. They had to walk from Auschwitz to Buchenwald in one long line of emaciated prisoners. They knew the frigid journey was a walk toward their death.

Wiesel was eventually rescued from Buchenwald by the Allied forces, but they came too late for his father. Only days earlier, he had died.

Memories of these experiences are no doubt the impetus for Wiesel's lifelong investment in ensuring such tragedy never repeats itself. Oddly enough, even through the horrors of Auschwitz and Buchenwald, Wiesel insists that he has maintained his faith in the existence of God.

One reporter who simply could not believe that Wiesel still believed in God asked him how we could reconcile the existence of a good God with the evil he had witnessed. This was Wiesel's reply.

> I have never forsaken [my faith], and it has never forsaken me. Whatever has been shaken has been shaken within faith, for faith has always been present. The question was: what is happening in the world, why is it happening, and according to what design? So, yes, there is a shaking of faith, but there is also faith.[1]

On another occasion Wiesel spoke openly about asking God why he would allow such a catastrophe. "I have not answered that question," he said to a reporter, "but I have not lost faith in God. I have moments of anger and protest." Then he says something remarkable. "Sometimes [in those moments of anger and protest] I've been closer to him for that reason [alone]."[2]

I don't presume to understand the degree of suffering and misery that Elie Wiesel endured and witnessed in the dual terrors of Auschwitz and Buchenwald. I'm not even sure I would have had the moral fortitude to maintain my belief through such pain. But I somehow understand what he means when he says, "Whatever has been shaken has been shaken within faith."

Even in my own doubts and in my own frustration with the way God's plan for my life has worked out, I somehow have always known in my heart of hearts that God was there, that he was at work, and that he cared about me. Even when dust was being shaken from the rafters of my faith, I somehow believed. Even when I wanted to run away in protest, and even when I was confused and frustrated, I felt the gravitational pull of my settled belief in the existence of a good God. He was just there and had always been there. Even if I was interested in letting go of him, he had no interest in letting go of me. When I couldn't begin to discern why some things were happening, I somehow knew who had everything under control.

When I take a moment to listen to what my heart is telling me, I realize that my doubts were also exercised *within* my belief and not against it. My faith was actually never at risk, even when it seemed to be on a respirator.

How I Came to Believe in God

Most people in the world believe in some sort of God, and they believe in God for all sorts of reasons. For me, it was ultimately a rational decision. I couldn't get past the old argument of the thirteenth-century philosopher and theologian Thomas Aquinas. He believed that God must exist because long ago, before history began, someone had to be without a beginning in order to create something out of nothing. Philosophers refer to this as the cosmological argument for the existence of God. They say at some point, an *uncaused cause* or a *first cause* initiated everything that we now know.

There are many other arguments for the existence of God—like the fact that I got through college or found my beautiful wife—but Aquinas' argument has always been the most compelling to me. In the end, this single argument did me in. I just couldn't meander my way around a simple question: How did everything begin? How did life come from nothing?

To this day, contemplating this just blows my mind, and it convinces me of the probable existence of God. If I am going to be intellectually honest with myself, laying all my presuppositions aside, I have to admit that the best explanation for this uncaused cause, based on all the information available to me, is that there was a supernatural creator who had no beginning. I call him God.

Simple enough, right? The existence of God makes sense. Once I settled into this belief, I asked myself a second question. If I believe God exists, then who is this God? This question has required much more deliberation.

From my childhood, I was taught to believe that this God was the God of the Bible, but my doubt caused me to look for other potential explanations for God. I wanted to determine which of the world's definitions of God was most likely to be true.

This long and arduous search could occupy another book. It took me into the heart of faiths like Hinduism, Buddhism, Islam, Sikhism, and Jainism and into many of their various sects and forms. I travelled to the holiest Hindu city, visited the site of Buddha's first sermon, stood in Asia's largest mosque, and toured many places mentioned in the Bible. I walked cremation grounds, met with Tibetan monks, and I even witnessed a man being exorcised of demons by a deceased Sufi saint. I read their texts, spoke to their leaders, visited their holy places, and dared to put my own prejudices aside. As I searched, within the quiet confines of my heart I dared to ask, what if this is the truth? What if Shiva, Allah, or Buddha is a better explanation than Jesus?

In the end, and without filling in all the gaps, I had to admit that no explanation of God, no religious system, and no holy person compared with Jesus, the God of the Bible. Eventually, my mind joined my heart and compelled me to believe in him.

God Is Defined, so Belief Is Demanded

When I decided the God of the Bible was the best explanation of God I could find, I had a choice to make. I could trust him or not. I could submit my will to him as God, or I could rebel against him, my Creator.

There is a problem with believing in the one true God. You simply can't come to him on your own personal terms. Because he is God, he is, by definition, in charge. He makes the rules, he calls the shots, and he deserves to be the master of your destiny. If he is God, he is also the boss. There is no boss of God. Discovering that he is God determines what I ought to believe and how I ought to live.

This is what the Bible refers to as *truth*. Truth is God's definition of what is right and just and his explanation of how we should live and perceive reality. This is what Jesus had in mind when he explained that if we hold to his teaching, we will know the truth, and the truth will make us free.

I have to resolve that I am inferior to God, who defines truth. My responsibility is to submit to his authority, to relinquish my desire to his control, and to channel my interests to serve his interests.

So I can choose to believe and to live those beliefs. Otherwise, I am by default choosing to rebel against those beliefs. In that case, I'm not rebelling against my mom or my dad or my teacher or my pastor. I'm rebelling against my Maker, who happens to also care deeply about me. This makes unbelief a double tragedy. I turn my back not only on my Creator but also on one who loves me more than I will ever be able to comprehend.

When I choose to believe in God, I don't get to choose what I want to believe, and I don't get to decide what truth is worth believing. I choose *whom* to believe, and he gets to tell me *what* to believe.

Typically, we do the exact opposite. We decide what we want to believe and then go about trying to redefine God (or find another god) to fit into our already established belief system. We put the cart before the horse.

This is epidemic today. People want to define truth for themselves, but it doesn't work that way. Defining the truth is not our job. That is God's job. Our responsibility is to believe and to live the truth that God defines. And in the end, when I believe the truth and live the truth, I find that truth helps me; it doesn't hurt me. This is what Jesus meant when he said that truth makes us free.

Settling This Question

Maybe you will also comb through the world's religions to seek the answers to your questions. As you do, I am convinced you will slowly begin to put to death your nagging questions and find good intellectual reasons to trust in Jesus Christ. But eventually, you have to make a decision about what you will believe. Will you choose to trust in God and accept his truth, or will you deny it?

Arrows of doubt ricocheted off my parents' divorce and lodged in me. In order to heal, I didn't need to answer intellectual questions about God; I needed to choose to trust him. I might have said during the most painful moments, "I don't even believe God exists anymore." But if I had diagnosed my wounds more clearly and spoken more honestly, I would have said, "I'm not happy with God right now." I didn't feel good about God. The logical reasons to believe never changed. My conviction was often still sturdy in my heart of hearts, and down deep inside I somehow knew God existed, but I wasn't willing to trust him in my season of personal pain.

If you decide to accept God as the source of truth, you're deciding to trust him.

When people repent of their sins and receive salvation in Jesus Christ, they make a choice to align their lives and their values with God. They leave their sin and rebellion, accept Jesus' gift of salvation, and begin to follow a new path of trust in God.

People often make a critical mistake when deciding whether to trust God: They wait until they *feel* like making the choice to totally follow him. Yes, this decision is sometimes an emotional one, but sometimes it is not. Choices are choices. You evaluate the evidence and make a choice.

So I'll invite you to ask yourself a few simple questions. If you don't trust God, do you know why? Do you know what keeps you from making the choice to believe? Is your doubt based on legitimate questions, or are you reluctant to give in to what you actually already believe?

Belief is eventually a decision, and I think people make that decision in two ways. One way is to slide into belief like a little kid who is nervous about getting into a swimming pool. He gets in the pool eventually, toe by toe and limb by limb, but it takes a long time. The other way is to jump into belief like a kid who backs up from the edge of the pool and then takes off running at full speed, hurtling himself into the pool without looking back.

When it comes to belief, some of us are sliders and some of us are jumpers. Neither is wrong, but eventually we have to decide whether we're going to get into the pool. We can't live half in and half out forever.

May I make a suggestion? If you are sliding in cautiously, why not just stop fighting and jump in?

Do you remember nervously dancing around the edge of the pool, wanting so badly to get in but still being afraid of the water? And do you remember what it was like when you finally had the courage to immerse yourself? It was so cold and uncomfortable—at first. But in seconds, everything changed. The chill went away, and you had the time of your life.

If you're beginning to sense that you're fighting against the God you know you need, maybe it would be liberating to simply stop. Maybe now is the moment to get on your knees and whisper a simple prayer— "God, I trust you."

That prayer might feel like a light rain on a searing summer day. And after it, everything changes.

BELIEF IN THE ASHES OF GENOCIDE
HOW EVEN EVIL SUPPORTS BELIEF

n 1994, more than a million Rwandans were murdered in barely more than 100 days. The sudden and mysterious assassination of Rwandan president Juvenal Habyarimana let the lid off of the steaming caldron of ethnic rivalry that had been brewing for many years in this tiny, beautiful nation in East Africa.

The tension between the Hutus and Tutsis had led to other skirmishes throughout Rwanda's tenuous history, but on this fateful occasion, it boiled over. The scalding hatred burned this tiny nation from corner to corner. In the end, many of the Tutsis were slain at the hands of their Hutu neighbors, and the weapon of choice in this genocide was a simple machete.

People were literally hacked to death while the modern world watched. Unadulterated hatred played itself out on a global stage with a cast of modern people who had promised to never let this sort of thing happen again. But it did happen again—while the world slept or watched it on the evening news. Evil ran amok, leaving orphans and widows and blood in its wake.

Within days, the victims' bodies were piled to rot in mass graves. Some churches became slaughterhouses with their pastors as coconspirators. Almost no one believed that Rwanda would ever recover from its gruesome moment in history. In a little more than three months, the nation became a place of the dead and their killers. Brave reporters and NGO workers have chronicled much of the genocide, and eyewitnesses continue to nurse deep psychological scars.

The victims were men, women, and even their children. The crime was simply being born a Tutsi, and the punishment was horrific and gruesome.

The general who was in charge of the United Nations mission in Rwanda, Roméo Dallaire, wrote an excruciating memoir in which he recounted stories of pregnant women being raped and their unborn children cut out of their stomachs as men were forced to watch. Murdering someone with a machete is hard work, according to Dallaire, so sometimes the murderers would leave their victims half dead and then come back the next day to finish the job. All night the victims would suffer in pain, lying among dead bodies, waiting for their own murder but too weak to escape. General Dallaire saw this gruesome story unfold. His memories of the massacre eventually became so overwhelming that he twice attempted suicide.

When I visited Rwanda, I stood on a hill overlooking a mass grave of a quarter of a million people. I visited a village church where 1500 people ran for refuge before being hacked to death inside. In the basement of the church I stood next to the entombed bones of 29,000 victims from the neighboring village. Many of those victims were children who were studying in the village school when the perpetrators arrived with their machetes and their blood lust.

Every living person I met was personally affected and deeply wounded by what had happened in this tiny East African country. If they didn't bear the physical scars of their near misses, they were haunted by the memory of watching their relatives' murders.

Choosing to trust God with the pain sparked by my parents' divorce was one thing. For people in Rwanda to trust him is a whole different thing.

My visit to Rwanda was not my first tryst with genocide. One year earlier, I spent a week in Bosnia facilitating a humanitarian project with some students from Liberty University. They stayed in the homes of local Bosnians, many with walls that were still peppered with holes from the bullets that sprayed their city during a three-year siege by the armies of Slobodan Milosevic. Everyone in this Bosnian city had his or her own story of loss from the genocide that occurred around the same time as the Rwandan incident.

I particularly remember having a long conversation with an elderly disabled man in a retirement home. He had been crippled his entire life, and until the genocide, he had lived in the same village his family had occupied for decades.

Then the killing began. As the soldiers marched from village to village, the old man knew that death awaited him, so he opted to kill himself rather than waiting for the Serbian soldiers to slice his neck. The soldiers wouldn't care that his disability made him nearly defenseless. They might kill him simply out of fear of their generals, or they might be personally convinced that the genocide was correct. Either way, he knew he would die slowly and painfully, as if the soldiers enjoyed it.

He resolved to kill himself so he wouldn't have to endure the torture. The gentle old man showed me the scar where he had taken a knife to his arm.

I'm fairly good at keeping my emotions at bay, but in this moment, I felt emotion well up inside of me. I had to step out of the room to collect myself. The man had told me how he survived his suicide attempt, and he explained that some fleeing neighbors took him to a safer place. He is a genocide survivor, but like all Bosnians, he has his own personal scar—a reminder of the moment he was cast in a real-life horror movie.

Most of the Bosnians living in his village were not so fortunate. They were murdered—relentlessly, painfully, and often slowly.

What I most remember about this man was his kind face and the warmth of our conversation. Despite communicating through a translator, I felt as if he were my own grandfather. He had a happy and welcoming face, and he was genuinely interested in me.

He was a victim of the unadulterated evil. He didn't deserve it, but it had happened. He didn't cause it, but he bore its repercussions.

Just before leaving Bosnia, we visited a bridge in a neighboring city. The bridge was built centuries earlier by the Ottoman Empire. It reached across a canyon that a river had carved out of the mountains. This bridge became the wicked set for a reincarnation of the Middle Ages.

More than 1000 Bosnian men had been collected from the village. Their necks were sliced, and they were thrown in the raging river below to die. These fathers and brothers were not soldiers; they were civilians who were simply guilty of being Bosnian. In a split second they died a needless death, their wives were widowed, and their children were orphaned.

I have since thought many times about what happened there. The memory is dog-eared in my mind as a reminder of what evil does to good people.

My final memory of Bosnia is of a gorgeous drive we took over a beautiful mountain. Pure white snow covered everything, including the branches of the mythical, slender trees that lined the roadside. The exquisite view was almost unearthly.

Then I thought about the genocide. I imagined the blood of innocent men and women painting that pure snow in crimson red. I could not believe so many good men had been murdered and so many good men had been deceived into believing that the Bosnians should be wiped from the earth.

Looking out the window for a moment with my head perched on my hand, I felt a deep, crippling sense of irony that something so horrific could have happened in such an enchanting place. I had no idea this kind of incarnate evil existed in our modern world.

How Evil Reveals God

I am writing this chapter from a hotel lobby in a typical American city filled with typical American people who can't begin to imagine genocide. They are just clueless. On their worst days, when they have no money and no love, they are still residents of the world's most prosperous, safe, and secure nation.

I just started crying. Right here in the hotel lobby, I'm crying. In fact, I'm a wreck. It's a little embarrassing, but I don't care. I've seen something worth crying about. Though I've never experienced war or genocide firsthand, I have seen its evidence, and that affected me deeply. Writing these words has reminded me of it.

The Archbishop of Rwanda told me that three years of ministry and therapy are normally required to get young genocide survivors to smile. They are so scarred by what they have experenced. They walk every day on ground fertilized by decaying human flesh. They weep 15-year-old tears as they recall the moments of incapacitating fear and wonder when their present security will be shattered again by a haunting reprise of latent, stewing hate.

Most people simply have no clue about the kind of evil that roams in parts of this world and in the hearts of certain men. In fact, I've heard some people say that evil is only a figment of our imagination. Only people who have never seen its effects make this absurd assertion. They are either misguided in their theology or oblivious of the reality gripping billions of people in need. They believe that all war and violence is unjust and that they are responsible to protest until peace blankets the earth. They try to find the good in even the worst things.

The only problem with this thinking is that people are still dying, evil men are still triumphing, and the world is still filled with injustice. Children are forced into slavery or prostitution, good people die needless deaths, and pain is the world's cheapest commodity.

I used to dabble with this kind of idealism. I went through my own phase where I danced with a looser kind of theology that sought to redefine evil as some form of misaligned good intention. The books I read propagated a softer kind of Christianity that was inclined toward pluralism and humanitarianism to the exclusion of the gospel. They were proponents of peace more than they were of Jesus. They also struggled with doubts about the accuracy of Scripture, and they questioned the veracity of the claims of Christ.

These new theologians' idealism looks suspiciously like an attempt to define truth for themselves. They went shopping to find a new kind of Christianity that fit their preestablished beliefs. They reinvented Jesus. They crammed Jesus into a kind of faith they were creating. This is why they didn't believe in evil, in genocide, and in the reality of the horror faced by men and women in places like Rwanda and Bosnia.

I was struggling with doubt and hypocrisy within the church, so I found some of their ideas to be interesting. But I was also struggling to submit to God's truth as the truth. I wanted to believe that sin and evil were overstated.

Then I witnessed the effects of the worst kind of sin and the evidence of overt demonic evil.

I wanted to believe that truth was a little flexible. That it was true for you or true for me but not absolute. Then I saw what happens when people act on what is true for them. I saw it in the tired eyes of people whom other people thought should be extinguished from the earth.

I wanted to believe that there wasn't a hell. Then I stood in the charred remains of hell on earth. I wanted to believe that when all was said and done, God would just roll out the red carpet into heaven and let everyone come, repentant or not. Then I read about or witnessed the work of men who could care less about God or man, and I saw how sin ends ultimately in the worst kind of death.

In his book on the Rwandan genocide, General Roméo Dallaire says something that I also came to believe. "I know there is a God because in Rwanda I shook hands with the devil. I have seen him, I have smelled him, and I have touched him. I know the devil exists, and therefore I know there is a God."

I don't know if Roméo Dallaire is a Christian, but I think his two-sentence argument for the existence of God is spot on. If evil exists, good must exist as well. Otherwise, we wouldn't know what evil is.

Ironically, it was the existence of evil that also helped lead C.S. Lewis to believe in God.

> If there is evil…there must be an…absolute "outside the world"…by which we can know it to be really evil. If there is real evil, then we must have a…standard of good by which we judge it to be evil. This absolute standard of goodness suggests a God who is himself this absolute, infinite standard.[1]

This search led Lewis to his belief in a moral law, made by God, that governs the ethics of the universe. Lewis combed through ancient history and studied great civilizations, including Egypt, Babylon, India, China, Greece, and Rome. He could not find a single example of a different kind of morality governing those civilizations. Lewis once wrote, "Think of a civilization where people were admired for running away in battle, or where a man felt proud of double crossing all the people who had been kindest to him. You might as well try to imagine a country where two and two made five."[2] Lewis determined that God must exist because there is a moral law, instituted by a divine being, that is somehow written on our hearts and in history. Evil is, by definition, the breaking of this moral law, and it is the opposite of God, not the work of God.

Why do we struggle to solidify our beliefs and build a bridge from those beliefs to our daily lives? One reason is that we have witnessed too little suffering and too little evil. As a result, we haven't acknowledged that God's truth leads to good. We haven't acknowledged our need for God. We haven't submitted to him who is the equilibrium of the universe.

Rwanda Finds God

My experiences in Rwanda and Bosnia led me to believe that there is good and there is evil. There is a God, and there is a devil. One path leads to life, and the other leads to destruction.

Today, people in Rwanda know they need God, and they have reached out to Jesus by the masses. Jesus is not well known in Bosnia. Consequently, Rwanda is miraculously recovering, but Bosnia is struggling to find her Prince of Peace. Many Rwandans know that Jesus heals wounded people and forgives sinners—even repentant perpetrators of genocide.

Many of the people I met in Rwanda had come to the end of their options and had found that Jesus was their only hope. Nearly everyone had difficult questions to ask God, but eventually they went after God for those answers. They knew they could decide to follow the path of evil, which would eventually lead to vengeance and more war and more death, or they could still believe and trust in a good God who could somehow repair the effects of the evil choices of deceived and depraved men.

Many of the Rwandans I met knew that only God could heal their wounded hearts, only God could pacify future hate, and only God could resurrect them from their ashes. They were too desperate to ask why God allowed their suffering. They just knew that only God could heal them.

Jesus Heals

Life hurts everyone, and everyone suffers in his or her own context. Few people will ever face the horror of genocide, but all of us have our own pain, our own wounds to nurse, and our own moments when we run to God in desperation or run away from him in distress. In those moments, we will choose to be either wounded and healing or wounded and hurting. Rwanda taught me not only about the evil of the enemy but also about the goodness and faithfulness of God.

John Rucyahana has been called "the Bishop of Rwanda." As I flew toward his nation, I read his book. He introduces the book by asking, where was God in Rwanda?

> In 1994, at least 1,117,000 innocent people were massacred in a horrible genocide in Rwanda, my homeland in central Africa. We are still finding bodies—buried in pits, dumped in rivers, chopped in pieces. Besides providing the details of this very sad story, my goal with this book is to tell an amazing, uplifting story. It is the story of the new Rwanda, a country that has turned to God, and which God is blessing.
>
> It is wrong to say that Rwanda was forgotten or hated by God. That is like saying that God forgot Jesus when He was on the cross. Jesus cried out in pain because He felt forsaken, but God had not forsaken Him. God was with Him in His pain, helping Him to achieve His purpose through that pain. Rwanda was abandoned and forgotten by the world, especially by the rich and powerful nations, but God did not forget Rwanda.
>
> Where was God when a million innocent people were being butchered?
>
> Where was God when priests and pastors helped massacre the people in their churches?
>
> I'll tell you where God was. He was alongside the victims

lying on the cold stone floor of the cathedral. He was comforting a dying child. He was crying at the altar. But He
was also saving lives. Many were saved by miracles. God
does not flee when evil takes over a nation. He speaks to
those who are still listening, He eases the pain of the suffering, and He saves those who can be saved. Man has a free
will, and God will not override it. Sometimes evil has its
day because men have so turned themselves over to it. But
even then, God does not abandon them. God waits to perform a miracle.

God waited for every moment during the genocide when
we would allow Him to work. For some, that happened in
an amazing way right under the devil's nose, but for most
of us it is happening now as God heals broken hearts and
seared consciences. God has always used the broken, and
He is using this broken nation to manifest His grace
and power. He is taking the brokenness caused by evil and
using it for a greater purpose—a great reconciliation in a
nation that the world had not only given up on, but had
given over to the devil, and its own evil.

I am not preaching such things from an isolated altar far
away from the conflict and oblivious to the pain. I speak
from Rwanda, and I speak through my own pain. My six-
teen-year-old niece, whom I dearly loved, was raped and
killed in a torturous, horrible way…I know what it is to
forgive through the tears.[3]

Healing

Bishop John Rucyahana invited me to deliver the Sunday homily
in his church. Honestly, I had no idea what to say. I prayed desperately
for God to help me. I felt like a nursing student tasked with performing open-heart surgery. I was unequipped.

I asked God to give me the words; I begged him for them. I knew
that many of those in the congregation were still struggling with
recessed pain, and some of them must have harbored a deep mistrust

in Christianity after witnessing many pastors' collaboration in Rwanda's genocide.

Even as hundreds of Rwandans piled into the cathedral, my heart was beating out of my chest. I was flipping nervously through the Bible, looking from side to side, and begging God to speak through me, past the language barrier and into the hearts of my Rwandan brothers and sisters.

God did help me, but my sermon wasn't the most memorable of my experiences in Bishop Rucyahana's church. In the middle of the service, I realized that those in attendance were both perpetrators of the genocide and their surviving victims. The murderers were worshipping with the hunted. The Hutus and the Tutsis were singing together in the presence of each other and of Jesus.

Bishop Rucyahana had spent much of his ministry preaching the power of the gospel to reconcile, and I was in the presence of it. The Christians there believed that Jesus forgives sin and heals hearts and can birth glorious things in very broken places.

This church was filled with healing people. Only by the power of God were they able to find their lost joy, and only by the power of God were they able to forgive each other and forgive themselves. Watching these men and women heal and worship together somehow quieted my nagging questions. My concerns looked so insignificant in this divine moment. I was staring at a parting of the Red Sea. The water of brokenness had morphed into the wine of healing, and the lion of revenge was lying down with the lamb of mercy. God was there in the ashes of destruction. He was not complicit in the genocide, but he was complicit in the people's healing.

These men and women knew that the world's greatest evil could not withstand the reconciling power of the gospel of Jesus Christ. So they worshipped their Healer at the top of their lungs. They clapped and raised their hands in praise. Their faces were adorned with magnificent smiles, and they were emulating joy. I could sense the power of new life in Christ.

Then, in a moment fit for an epic, the Christians concluded the Sunday service by singing "It Is Well with My Soul." I knew then that

I needed to better know *this* Jesus. This Jesus wasn't just a historical figure to the Rwandans. He was resurrected and alive, and he was at work in turning their ashes into something beautiful. This wasn't the Jesus of fake, cultural Christianity. This was the Jesus who makes water spring to life in barren places. The Jesus who imagined the Sahara Desert and the San Andreas Fault, who thought up love, and who turns water into wine. I needed more of *that* Jesus in my life.

WE ARE ALL ORPHANS
SEEING JESUS IN FULL COLOR

We struggle to believe and to live out our beliefs because we have never seen Jesus binding up the brokenhearted, healing and helping broken people. We live our Christianity as if Jesus were still in his tomb.

In fact, every time we crawl back under our layers of manicured, cultural Christianity, we are entombing Jesus again. We roll the stone of apathy over the door that leads to a living, breathing, life-changing, helping, healing Jesus. We barricade ourselves from the resurrected Jesus we so desperately need.

And if we do this enough, we substitute the real Jesus with a tame, bland, boring Jesus. He becomes like a black-and-white picture of a sunset. He isn't brilliantly alive in our minds or busily at work in our daily lives. He isn't healing us here and now; he becomes the Jesus of the then and there, just another character in another one of history's stories. Oddly, we have a knack for taking the most essential story in history and deconstructing it into another storied account from a different time.

But Jesus is not just another story! He is the hinge upon which history swings. His story is epic, the source of what we're looking for regardless of whether we know how desperately we need it. Jesus' story reveals to us what we actually need even if we don't want it or we think we need something else even more.

We don't know Jesus well. He is easily the most famous person in history—almost everyone is well acquainted with his story, many people believe in his deity and his resurrection, and all true believers have at some point pledged their lives in trust to him. But we don't know Jesus well because we have allowed our cultural Christianity to rub off his shimmer. We've let him fade into our memories, so we've become nominal, uncommitted, halfhearted, PR Christians. Life with God is reduced to a religious stunt.

Jesus is still admired for his teachings, and he's trusted for his sacrifice, but somehow his life and death don't seem as real anymore. So we read about Jesus the way we read a stale account of George Washington crossing the Delaware or Napoleon on his conquests. Reading about Jesus is not just spiritual homework. It is divine. It is alive.

Too Familiar

Part of the problem is that Jesus' story is so familiar to us. We know it so well that the life has been drained from it like the stories our grandfathers told us over and over.

Remember your grandfather's stories? The first time you heard them, you were fascinated. You laughed and you were perplexed, and maybe you even cried. But your grandfather told the same stories every Christmas for ten years, and you soon had them memorized. You anticipated the punch lines, and you knew what was coming next. They weren't interesting and surprising anymore. The wonder was sanded off by repetition.

But even without the wonder, you continued to listen because you so enjoyed your relationship with your grandfather. Long after the stories lost their fascination, you continued to enjoy those moments simply because you were with your grandfather. The stories were just a bridge between you and him. They were decorating the relationship. They were the pictures on the wall. They were the ornaments on the tree.

I've learned that the same thing is true when it comes to my relationship with God. I have to remember that the stories about Jesus are vehicles that take me to deeper places in my relationship with him. The relationship is bigger than just the stories.

I have to stay closely connected to Christ, or he will fade somewhere in the recesses of my mind, where I store the historical accounts I learned through my childhood. He'll sit right there next to the story of Shah Jahan's construction of the Taj Mahal and the delivery of the Statue of Liberty to the United States. Jesus will chill in my mind with Winston Churchill, Hudson Taylor, and Ghandi.

I have to view Jesus' story correctly, and I have to realize that the last chapter is still unwritten. Jesus' story is still being written today, in the world and my life, here and now. If I don't realize this, I'll be tempted to live through secondhand accounts of faith. I will never pursue my own deepening relationship, and my experience with him will be confined solely to other people's testimonies. The color will fade from my life with God, just as it does from the sun-worn furniture on the back deck of an old beach house. The sunrise will arrive again in black-and-white.

Jesus, the Grand Canyon, and Imagination

Our experience with Jesus can easily become like my experience with the Grand Canyon. As a child, I knew people who had visited the Grand Canyon, I had watched documentaries describing it, and I had gazed at pictures of it. I learned that it carves its way through the western United States for almost 300 miles, and at points it cuts a gash in the earth 15 miles wide and a mile deep. I learned that the great Colorado River looks like a trickling stream when you gaze down at it from the top of the canyon, and I learned that all of this is nestled in the middle of one of America's most barren and deserted places.

I learned all of this before I visited the Grand Canyon myself. I knew about it from secondhand accounts, but knowing about something and experiencing something are drastically different. I knew about the canyon, but it was all hearsay. I wasn't an eyewitness.

When I did finally visit it, I quickly realized that the stories I had heard and the images I had seen were vastly less impressive than the real thing. The Grand Canyon was just incomprehensible through firsthand knowledge. It was so much larger and so much more imposing than I could have imagined.

I'll never forget the day my dad and I finagled our way into a helicopter tour over the monstrosity. It was glorious. The moment I hovered over the Grand Canyon remains imprinted on my memory. I will tell my grandchildren about that moment. There is life in that memory because when I talk about it, I'm speaking from my own experience. It's a first-person story tied to a real event.

We should always be able to recount our own and our latest experiences with Jesus. Our stories should be in the first person, and they should come from firsthand knowledge.

When people ask us about Jesus, we could answer their questions by retelling other people's experiences with him. But how much better to answer their questions by retelling our own experiences with him! We can tell people about his work in our lives and about our personal love for him.

As our experiences with Jesus Christ grow, we more naturally and easily live the kind of lives we want to live and we know we need to live. We find the courage to believe. In fact, I've learned that having the power to live this kind of life is nearly impossible if I don't stay in close proximity to Jesus. I can much more easily believe and live the truths I know in my heart are true when I am serious about nurturing my relationship with him. In the next section, I'll write more about nurturing that relationship, but I'll give you a preview here.

I've learned that giving time to my relationship with Jesus and using my imagination are the two secrets that keep my relationship with him alive. No relationship grows without time, and your relationship with Jesus and the Bible will be immeasurably richer if you let your imagination help you witness the most important events of biblical history.

For instance, not too long ago, I read 2 Corinthians 8:9: "You know the grace of our Lord Jesus Christ, that though he was rich, yet for your sakes he became poor, so that you through his poverty might become rich." I first read it as a normal account of the gospel. I wasn't immediately compelled by it. I understood it to say, "Jesus came from heaven to a sin-saturated earth and suffered and died in my place." As I saw it, that's basically all Paul meant to say.

Then I stopped to meditate on the verse and apply my imagination to it. Almost immediately, a parable came to mind. It wasn't just the formulation of words in my head; it was a crystal-clear image. I could *see* the story play out in my mind, and the drama added electricity to that simple Bible verse. It came alive with blinking red lights and sirens. I was inside the verse; it had walked off the page and into my life. Instead of merely understanding words, I was staring at Jesus face-to-face.

I was standing in the Grand Canyon.

This parable gave new meaning to the message of a simple verse. It caused me to see it differently—in color and not in black-and-white. The parable made it come alive. This was a very personal and intimate moment in my relationship with God, but I'd like to share that parable with you.

The Parable That Colored In the Gospel

Anna has lived on the streets since her mother and her father left her at the train station. Right now, her house is a ditch. She guesses she's about ten.

Anna lives in an era before electricity and running water. Kings still ride in carriages, and court jesters are hit entertainers. Life's rhythm is measured by the sun rising and the sun setting. The poor are ever poorer, the richer are ever richer, and hope is the rarest of commodities. For some people—people like Anna—hope is impossible.

As an orphan, Anna has learned to fend for herself pretty well. She knows which houses throw out the best leftovers and which alleys are precarious for little girls at night. She is a good enough fighter to keep her food from the weaker street kids, and she is sly enough to hide it from the older ones. She is street savvy—a survivor.

She is also miserable.

Every new day seems to fuel her misery. She sleeps in her ditch, her one set of clothes is getting too small, and her hair has become impossibly long and matted with mud. Her skin is normally three shades darker than it should be because of the ash caked to it. She is always hungry, and she is tired of the way people look at her with disgust. Even worse are the patronizing glares of genuinely sympathetic people who are willing to stare but totally unwilling to help.

Worst of all, she is always afraid. She knows that it's only a matter of time before a thief or slave trader "invites" her to join his business. She knows that the horror she has known is nothing compared to what she will know. She is always scared with a spine-chilling fright that most people never know in real life. For her, fiction is her reality. She has no future, and she knows it.

She is a street kid. That's all she is, and that's all she will ever be.

Anna used to smile only once every year. The kingdom where she lived held an annual festival that was like something out of a storybook. The whole nation came alive with entertainment and feasting. Music and laughter filled the streets. A fantastic parade featured lines of carriages and clowns, exotic animals and entertainers, and even the king himself, who rode in the procession in his carriage of pure gold. Anna anticipated this parade every year. It was the only thing she had to look forward to. She would leave her ditch, climb atop a wall, and wait in anticipation for the parade to arrive.

First, she would hear the pounding of the drums and the whistling of the flutes. The music crescendoed as the parade came closer and closer, and what was left of the child in her laughed and laughed as she watched the clowns stumble and bumble along.

The animals fascinated her. She marveled at the serpentine neck of the giraffe and was stunned by the massive size of the elephant. One year, she even saw a cart of caged African lions. They slept in their cage for most of the parade, but she was fortunate enough to see them when they were awake. She still remembers watching them walk from one end of their tiny cage to the other. Each lion had the anxious gaze of a hunter ready for his prey.

For some reason, she thought it was funny. The lions looked so frustrated as they paced back and forth in their cage. She leaned over to tell someone how pretty she thought the lions' manes looked and how unusual it was that such a powerful and dangerous animal could be so beautiful.

But as usual, no one was there for her to tell. Loneliness washed over her. She dropped her head. But then she saw the clowns again, and she was immediately cheered by their antics.

Still, the clowns were not her favorite part of the parade. Neither were the animals or the music. She most anticipated catching a glimpse of the king's carriage. She had never seen anything else so beautiful in all her life.

So she waited and watched in anticipation. Eventually, she saw it in the distance, covered with gold and adorned in precious jewels that shined in the sun. It was beautiful and priceless, and she felt as if she were in a magical land where paupers could become princes and where everyone's dreams could come true. There were no orphans in her daydream.

Every once in a while, the good king would swing open the door of his carriage and wave at the cheering crowds. Anna loved it when he did this. The king had such a happy, kind face. Anna would wave and smile, pretending that the king was waving at *her*.

Always before, she waited all year for this moment—but not this year. Anna is just too miserable to care any longer about the parade. There is no joy left, no smile hidden in her heart. She can already hear the ruckus of the approaching parade when she decides to leave her wall and climb back into her ditch.

She rolls up into a little ball, her face buried in the sand and her back against the road. The parade will pass right by her. She will have a front-row seat, but she doesn't want it. She doesn't even have the strength to turn to catch a passing glimpse. She is just too sad. She wishes she could sleep her life away.

The parade goes by as Anna sleeps in her ditch. The court jesters and the clowns, the giraffe and the elephants, the musicians and a hundred other spectacles pass by so closely that their shadows shield Anna from the noonday sun.

Then the king's carriage arrives in its glimmering glory. Still, Anna sleeps.

The king opens the door, and the people cheer. Everyone clamors to catch a glimpse of his kind face as the chariot moves slowly through the center of the town. This has been the highlight of every parade.

But then something unusual happens. The king abruptly orders the carriage to stop, and everyone begins to wonder if something is wrong.

The king has followed this path a dozen times, and never in the history of the parade has he ever stopped here.

The rich folks on the side of the street straighten their clothes. Maybe he's coming to greet them!

One guy asks his friend, "Is something wrong?"

His friend, straightening his tie, replies "Oh no, he's probably coming to say hello to a wealthy patron." He hopes he's the one.

The king is a large and imposing man. He seems to fill up the street. The enormous train of his scarlet robe drags out of the carriage as he walks down the dusty road. The fabric is priceless. The scene seems a bit bizarre as the royal garment flops down onto the ground in a plume of dust. Even more strange is the sight of him walking down the street, dragging the robe in his wake. Its deep red color quickly fades under a coat of dust.

Anna is oblivious. She is still sleeping in her ditch.

But suddenly she is jarred awake by two large arms scooping underneath her. Fear runs up her spine. Is someone kidnapping her? Immediately Anna moves into survival mode. Her muscles tense. She begins to think more quickly. She cocks back her arm to strike and turns her head to zero in on her target.

Suddenly she stops in disbelief—the king has picked her up.

Horrified at the sight of her own filthy skin and clothes touching the king's beautiful robe, she is ashamed and confused.

He whispers to her, "It's okay," as he strides toward his carriage. Anna is speechless; the crowd is stunned. Gently, the king lifts her into the beautiful coach and orders his drivers to proceed.

From that moment on, Anna became a part of the king's family. She ate at his table and wore beautiful clothes. The king changed her life and her destiny because he adopted her into his family.

That's how Anna became the daughter of the king.

This is the kind of moment Jesus was imaging when he said in John 14:18, "I will not leave you as orphans; I will come to you." The apostle

Paul had this idea in mind when he wrote the verse I read and others like it.

"You know the grace of our Lord Jesus Christ, that though he was rich, yet for your sakes he became poor, so that you through his poverty might become rich."[1] "You were bought at a price."[2] "In love he predestined us to be adopted as his sons through Jesus Christ, in accordance with his pleasure and will."[3]

The Surprise Twist

What if Anna's story didn't have a happy ending? Imagine she arrived at the king's home and quickly set up a new life in her own private wing of the castle. But despite her new father's love, she refused to speak with him and to acclimate to her new life. In fact, she only came to dinner occasionally, and when she did come, she sat at the far end of the table. During the whole meal she refused to make conversation with her new father, the king. Sometimes she passed him while taking a morning stroll through the wide hallways of the castle, but even then she only nodded. She even complained that her new clothes weren't trendy and that her room was old-fashioned.

What if Anna ended up becoming an ungrateful brat? I revolt at the thought that she would neglect such generosity and refuse to communicate with the king. Yet I can see myself in the image of Anna as an ungrateful brat. My own indifference toward God's generous love looks all too similar.

We are recipients of great grace, so to intentionally or accidentally ignore our relationship with God is a tragedy in its most epic sense. We become Anna the brat, cordoned off in our own side of the castle, willfully ignoring our adoptive Father.

God certainly deserves our subjection because he is God, but something much deeper compels us to live faithfully. The apostle Paul says, "God's kindness leads you to repentance."[4] When we begin to really understand his love and grace, we are compelled to believe and to live faithfully. When I see Jesus as he is, I desire to live in a way pleasing to him. My gratitude fuels my relationship with him.

God has done more than enough to deserve our belief.

PART 2

FROM BELIEF TO A HEALTHY SOUL

I t's not enough to just admit that God is God and that he is sufficiently deserving of your belief. This is simply a first step that launches your relationship with him. In order to have a healthy relationship with God, you have to fill up your mind and your heart with his truth. Otherwise, you will never learn to honestly live what you believe. Your relationship with God will always be weak if you don't regularly consume truth, or if you become distracted by lesser things, or if you choose to rebel against what God says is true.

THE NECESSITY OF SOUL FOOD
THE EMACIATED SOUL

6

Weak Christians don't typically slam the door on God. Their commitment usually wanes through neglect and a slow, spiritual starvation. Your relationship with God is a lot like your relationship with other people. You have to put the right stuff into it to get the right stuff out of it.

Relationships rarely die because of one cataclysmic event. Relationships more often die by the combined effect of hundreds of little decisions to ignore the needs of other people, or to constantly prioritize your needs above their needs. Eventually, communication weakens between people. They don't chitchat "just because" anymore, and soon they avoid one another altogether. Before you know it, relationships that once were thriving will lie near death in the corners of rooms plastered with old memories of better days.

Why? Because relationships die by starvation. When they are fueled with the right things, they thrive. Dying relationships limp along on fading recollections of past joys. Healthy relationships are always creating new memories. The same will be true of your relationship with God. Chances are, if it's unhealthy, the problem has to do with spiritual starvation.

It Begins with My Stomach

Here's how I think about it. If I'm going to live, I have to eat, right? This is the basic premise undergirding my physical life: If I don't eat, I die. It's that simple. Dead people don't enjoy life very much, so I ought to eat if I'm going to enjoy life.

This principle is coming from my heart. I not only need to eat, I enjoy eating. You wouldn't know it from looking at me, but I am totally obsessed with food. I'm among the least likely people in the world to be hungry. I've been known to drive two hours one way in order to eat at one of my favorite restaurants. I have actually sat for hours, seemingly in a drug-induced state, fawning over those cheesy cooking shows. I especially love watching the travel versions in which overeager chefs go to the ends of the earth to eat ants and rats and feast on rotten fish, rattlesnakes, and cow brain. I have personally been coaxed into eating dog soup, boiled frog, chicken feet, and a cute little village goat.

Some folks call people like me *foodies* or *foodaholics*. And the truth is, I'm actually a junior varsity foodaholic. I know a few college students who are varsity foodaholics. They are 110-pound eating machines who would jump over a barbed wire fence on the back of their grandma for a chance to eat a filet mignon or, if they're from the South, a good, greasy bucket of fried chicken. You can picture them. They eat from dawn to dusk and still have the body fat of a European supermodel. They regularly wash down loads of saturated fat with 2000 calories of soda and somehow manage to look like their momma and daddy starved them when they were children. I'm sure that one day I'll be an old man at the beach, carrying around my Richard Simmons calorie counter, when a few of these superhumans will pass by me on their way to McDonalds. In their Speedos.

Of course, most people aren't *that* fanatical about food, but here's a settled fact—every living, breathing person has to eat, or he or she will die. It's just that simple.

I think the principle applies to our souls as well. If not eating is detrimental to my physical health, then not feeding my soul is detrimental for my spiritual health. If I don't feed my soul, or if I feed my soul wrongly, I will have an unhealthy, undernourished relationship with God. My relationship with God will begin to weaken by a slow starvation. This is why Jesus said, "Man does not live on bread alone, but on every word that comes from the mouth of God" (Matthew 4:4).

Why Do We Spiritually Starve Ourselves?

Prioritizing your spiritual health is difficult. If you're like me, taking in spiritual food rarely seems as important as eating three meals a day. Why is this so hard to get straight?

We starve ourselves spiritually for one of two primary reasons. First, in our heart of hearts, we don't perceive our spiritual health to be as important as our physical health. Second, we ignore our spiritual health accidentally as our other priorities shove it to the side. The first problem requires a shift in our attitude; somehow we have become arrogant enough to think we don't need God anymore. The second problem requires a shift in how we manage our time so that the regular pressures and distractions of daily life are kept in their proper place. Both issues require a long struggle to maintain humility and balance (more about this later).

You have invested some time and energy to read this far, so I probably don't have to convince you that this part of your life is worth the fight. Even people who appear to be uninterested in spiritual things have a hunch, down deep in their hearts, that these things are probably worth their attention. Something in our soul cries out on occasion and begs us to pay attention. We can try to push those thoughts out of our minds and hearts, we can try to bury them under piles and piles of other things, but somehow, something inside of us still tells us that this is important. That voice, those feelings inside, are like spiritual hunger pangs that were placed there by our Creator, God.

When we are spiritually unhealthy, we begin to feel this emptiness groaning on the inside. People sometimes misinterpret this emptiness as a hunger for something else and try to satiate it with all kinds of substitutes. They try to get a lot of money or notoriety, hoping these things will fill them up. They work to elevate their social status and to collect expensive things that other people wish they had, but somehow the emptiness is still there. Others will try to fill the echoing hollowness by doing nice things that make them feel good about themselves. They may embrace social justice and fight with all their might for the disenfranchised and underprivileged. Yet their soul still groans.

Having money or embracing justice are certainly not evil, but these pursuits alone will not satisfy the emptiness. The hunger pangs are actually from God, who is crying out for a personal relationship with you. If you have already given your life to Jesus, he is probably drawing you to a deeper relationship or calling you back after a distant season. The emptiness is sometimes God's way of inviting people to accept for the first time the gift of a restored relationship through Jesus' life, death, and resurrection.

All through history people have written of these groanings of the soul. They are a universally shared experience. John Calvin referred to them as the "seed of religion," and St. Augustine wrote in his *Confessions*, "Our hearts are restless till they find rest in Thee." Some people have called this emptiness a God-shaped hole in our hearts.[1] I think that's a good way of putting it.

I'm convinced that many times when we feel like something is off in our lives, that God-shaped hole is groaning. It shouts at us to feed our souls because they are starving.

Is Your Soul Groaning?

I wonder if that emptiness is crying out to you at this moment. Maybe that is the reason why you're holding this book. Maybe it asked you to read something like this. Maybe your soul is healthy and your relationship with God is alive. On the other hand, maybe you're on a spiritual respirator. Either way, your soul might be hungry, wanting more of something, feeling unsatisfied.

If you need to begin a relationship with Jesus, or you need to begin caring about your relationship again, you can do something about that in this very moment. Are you feeling jaded and disillusioned and ready for a change? Have you neglected your soul for some time but started feeling hunger pangs for God again? Maybe you're beginning to realize that you believe more than you've been willing to admit.

If you're feeling any of these things, I suggest you stop to pray right now. Go find some private place as quickly as you can and have a conversation with God. You don't have to carefully craft sentences dripping in holy prose. You can just roll what's on your mind onto God's shoulders and talk to him with the same frankness and deep honesty you would share with a friend.

Get on your knees, bow your head, and just tell your Father what you need to tell him. Confess what has gone wrong, ask for his help for a new beginning, and then get up, dust yourself off, and start doing what you need to do to get healthy again.

When you pray, talk to God as if you're in your living room with him. Don't imagine him sitting on a distant throne in a faraway land. Talk to him with the assurance that he's there with you at this very moment. When you're done, you can come back to this chapter.

Let Me Help You

Don't you feel better now that you've laid it all on the table? I've had experiences like this many times in my own relationship with God. Sometimes I'm like an unanchored ship slowly drifting off into the ocean. Every once in a while, I'm surprised to discover how far away I am from God, and I have to drop my anchor again. This is what these moments of honest prayer and soul searching do—they re-anchor your soul in a world where it can all too easily drift away from God.

If you weren't reading this book, and we were together having this conversation over coffee (as I wish we were), I would pull my chair a little closer to you at this moment. I'd prop my elbow up on the table, take a sip of my coffee, and make eye contact with you before speaking. I think if you looked in my eyes, you would be able to see my genuine concern.

I would say, "Doesn't it feel good to know things are okay with God again? Doesn't it feel good to stop the fight and just submit to him?"

And maybe you would reply, "It feels like a weight was just lifted off my shoulders."

I would agree. "God *has* lifted that weight off your shoulders, but I have to tell you, this is just the beginning. One good meal doesn't take care of you for good. You need a balanced diet. You have to learn to live this way. You have to feed yourself regularly."

If you're like a lot of people I've spoken with, you'd probably say, "I know you're right, but I don't know how to live this way. Can you help me?"

And of course, I would be willing to help you, and here's what I would prescribe.

Spiritual Life 101: How to Get a Balanced Diet

First, make space for God. Carve out, schedule, and commit to specific times in the week when you're going to give attention to your spiritual health. For me, it's every morning before dawn. I have friends who do this at night, or over lunch, or three mornings a week. There's no rule, but if you don't designate time for your soul, nothing will change. We'll consider this a little more in the next chapter.

Second, have regular examinations. You need to get honest with yourself and determine which aspects of your life need special attention. For instance, some people don't love God with their *mind* because they are plagued with factual doubts. These people should intentionally read books and listen to lectures that address their intellectual questions about their faith. They need to feed themselves information. Other people have endured serious suffering in their lives, and they need a good counselor to help them discern and interpret their pain. Revisit the weak areas of your life and determine which parts of you are crying out for attention. We all need some soul maintenance every few thousand miles.

Third, choose to change. The second step will reveal all kinds of things about you. Some of these things will embarrass you. Some will be easier to change than others. Some will call for only a slight adjustment, and others will require drastic change. Eventually you have to decide how important your spiritual life is to you. If it's really important to you, then you must do whatever it takes to nourish it, and I mean *whatever it takes*. Sometimes you have to take drastic measures to stay spiritually healthy. Take them.

Fourth, learn to listen to God. It's not enough to just read the Bible, listen to sermons, and immerse yourself in spiritual activity. The Bible says that God sometimes speaks in a still, small voice. I can't give you a formula to learn to listen to that voice, but the more you grow to know God, the more you'll learn to recognize his voice. When you hear it, listen. In the next chapter, I'll help you with this.

Fifth, eat well and eat regularly. No unhealthy person gets healthy overnight. The same is true for your soul. This will take time. The best thing you can do for yourself is to get in the habit of regularly digesting truth. Reading this book is a great step. Maybe you should also go to my website (www.johnniemoore.org) to look at some helpful resources and some videos I posted to help you in your path to spiritual health.

Finally, get passionate and get excited about this journey. Many times we approach our spiritual life with a depressed attitude. We are always dissatisfied with where we are. Often we know we need to change, and we feel the weight and pressure of it all, but this kind of attitude doesn't help us change. It actually hurts us. You need to choose to be passionate and excited about this journey.

Eat, Eat, Eat

Earlier, I confessed to you that I'm a foodaholic. While I'm eating lunch, I'm thinking about dinner, and while I'm eating dinner, I'm thinking about the next day's breakfast. When I arrive at a restaurant, I already know what I'm going to order. I would be more likely to walk over the Grand Canyon on a tightrope than skip the opportunity to eat one of my favorite meals at one of my favorite places…especially if the restaurant was on the other end of that tightrope!

Sometimes I wonder what it would be like if I were this passionate, this determined, this energetic, and this anticipatory about feeding my soul. This morning I received a glimpse of this kind of passion and determination when I was reading in the book of Luke. Luke describes a moment when Jesus encountered a paralyzed man.

The story begins with Jesus attracting yet another crowd. People inflicted with all kinds of ailments and handicaps had gathered in droves in and around a small house. The whole scene was chaotic. It was musty and crowded, and there wasn't a square inch of remaining space. People were pushing and pulling and squeezing and funneling impossibly out of the entrance of some guy's house that Jesus had converted into a makeshift classroom-hospital.

In the crowd was a group of men who had decided to bring their paralyzed friend to Jesus. We don't know anything about that paralyzed man except that he wouldn't have made it to Jesus had his friends not helped him get there.

These men might have walked for miles to transport their friend to Jesus' emergency room, but when they arrived, they found the little house impossibly full. I can imagine that the heart of the paralyzed man sank. As he looked at the enormous crowd, he realized they would not be getting anywhere near Jesus. How could he be so close to hope and yet still so far away?

Just then one of his determined friends had a wild idea. He decided they should scale the house and drop inside through the roof. It was risky, but it was their only option. One guy grabbed a rope, and another found a ladder. Soon the whole crew had scaled the wall of the house, and they heaved and pulled until they were able to pull their friend to the roof on his mat.

Immediately, the man's friends started ripping tiles off the roof of the house.

What did people inside the house think? Tiles were crashing on the ground in plumes of dust. The friends knew they had to work quickly before someone stopped them, so they ripped off the tiles with furor and hurled them to the hardened dirt underneath them. The whole thing was an insane mess, like a cymbal crash in the middle of a wedding.

Then the first beam of sunlight poked through the shattering roof, revealing a million little dust particles. They knew they were close. The tempo of the work increased, as did the pounding of the paralyzed man's heart.

Everyone inside the house was either worried at the racket or angered by the impetuousness of these men—that is, everyone but Jesus. He just smiled. He got a kick out of their tenacity and admired their determination. He was having a hard time containing his laughter as he watched the whole scenario unfold. He watched the uptight people get angrier, and he heard the noise of the man's frantic friends ripping off the roof of the house. And he watched as they lowered their paralyzed friend through the hole they had created.

Did Jesus wish his disciples were this dedicated to him? Did he know that in the not-too-distant future, they wouldn't even stay awake to pray with him or hang around to watch his trial?

Finally the man landed on the floor. He crashed in a splash of dust right in front of Jesus, almost lying on his toes. He was delirious with anticipation. Would the angry people in the house beat him? Or would Jesus heal him? He covered his head, half in shame and half in fear.

But Jesus had already decided he would heal the man. In only a few seconds, the divine Creator and a broken, paralyzed man shared a transaction. The muscles in the paralytic's legs retracted and contracted as the same power that first breathed life into Adam in the Garden of Eden pulsed through his atrophied limbs. He stood up for the first time. His legs were wobbling, but he smiled with the kind of smile that hurts your cheeks. He started clapping and screaming and thanking Jesus over and over.

His body wasn't the only thing that was healed. His destiny was changed.

When I read this story again this morning, I was most affected by one simple thought: When someone encounters Jesus, things change.

That man's friends could have given up and left. Instead, they pressed on to get closer to Jesus. They decided to do whatever was necessary. They believed this was their only hope, so they were determined. And because of their refusal to be denied, their friend left changed. We too must come to the place where we realize that Jesus is our only hope, and then we must press on toward him with determination as those men did.

What if we became truly determined to get spiritually healthy, and what if we chose to run after Jesus like this? Ultimately, having a healthy soul rests on the other side of determination—determination to digest truth and live it out, the kind of determination that's willing to rip off a roof if necessary.

TUNING YOUR EARS TO THE VOICE OF GOD
THE DISTRACTED SOUL

7

If ever someone had the potential to be a madly successful multitasker, surely Jesus did. For one thing, he created the world. He sculpted the Himalayas, formed and ripped apart the continents, imagined and painted the heavens, and for our viewing pleasure, granted us ten billion sunsets and sunrises to make their daily dance in the sky.

History is Jesus' puppet. DNA and black holes might have been mere afterthoughts. And his book is still the world's bestseller. He created a world that is both massive and delicate, and his inventions make Thomas Edison's look like fifth-grade science projects.

Jesus dreamed up our brains, for instance. They weigh in at only three pounds, yet they house 100 trillion connections between 100 billion neurons. A few weeks ago I watched an online video of a scientist lecturing on the evolution of the Internet. He said that the complexity and interconnectedness of the whole world's Internet in 2005 was roughly equivalent to one human brain!

Jesus made that.

If I made the world and then came to visit my planet, I would have lived my life like a superhero. Convincing people that they needed to pay attention to me would be hard work. It wouldn't always be fun or rewarding, so I would probably play hard at night to let off some stress. I'd fly through the sky, drink a gallon of Dead Sea water, play jokes on the Pharisees while they were sleeping, and set every record in every existing sport. I'd have the fastest horse in the hippodrome, win every gold medal in the Olympics, and enjoy a little soccer game on the Sea of Galilee.

In other words, if I were Jesus, I would be a show-off. I'd heal everyone. I would part rivers regularly. I would turn King Herod into a donkey or give wings to camels. And I would have made a spectacle of the false teachers who tried to deceive my followers. I would have been like Harry Potter on acid, and I might have made all my spectacles ticketed events and then used the revenue to finance my church-planting efforts around Galilee.

If I were Jesus, I certainly wouldn't have wasted my valuable time sitting in the lilies, thinking and praying. Yet for some reason, Jesus spent a lot of time sitting in the lilies and praying.

I'm amazed when I consider what Jesus valued and how he used his time. He wasn't impressed with notoriety or popularity, he didn't show off, and he was more interested in impressing the widow and the orphan than the rich and powerful. Evidently, he also regularly snuck away. "Jesus often withdrew to lonely places and prayed" (Luke 5:16). He was *always* doing this.

This is the same Jesus who dreamed up a single star that is 250 million miles in diameter. The same Jesus who dreamed up a sun to heat the earth—a sun that is large enough to contain more than a million earths and four million moons. The same Jesus who created an immeasurable number of infinitesimal cells, each somehow containing three billion letters of information in its nucleus.

That same Jesus took time to get away, to rest, and to pray. He didn't have to. He was God. But he chose to.

Jesus intentionally and regularly paused to breathe, pray, and nurture his relationship with God. He turned off all outside influences with regularity so he didn't lose control of his mission or of his daily life.

I suppose it's logical then that since we're not God, we probably need to do the same. We need to choose to get away and spend time with God. Otherwise, we'll be gasping for spiritual air.

How often do *you* do this? If you're like me, you probably have an incredibly hard time slowing down and chilling with your Maker. It's hard to unplug from the digital age and just rest. But if we don't take the time to rest in God's presence, we're sending a message to Jesus that we think we're somehow better and stronger than he is.

Press the Pause Button

I once heard a wise old man say, "Look at the way you use your time, and you'll know what's most important to you." He was not talking about his soul, but I think the advice applies just the same. If you're going to get close to Jesus, if you're going to feed your relationship with God and have a healthy soul, if you're going to honestly live what you believe, you're going to have to put time and effort into it.

But if you're like me, you usually pay particular attention to everything else in your life and leave your soul maintenance to your excess time and excess energy. After all, you have bills to pay and classes to take and relationships to nurture and life to live. Life is busy and full of pressures, and somehow God always gets pushed to the margins.

We may be serious about God, but we are also very serious about a lot of other things. We have to pay attention to our education and our career, our relationships and our physical health. Soon we get caught in the rhythm of life, and eventually we're turning our attention to God only when we're desperate or when the emptiness gets unbearable again.

We get busy, and when we're too busy, we care about God only when we're laid off or our relationship crumbles or we have no one else to call on for help. You know how it is. Suddenly we see one of life's storms approaching and hear the thunder clapping. We wake up our latent religion, rustle up our Bible, dust it off, and start praying in desperation. Actually, we're treating God as our last-ditch effort after exhausting all our other options.

Then, once the crisis is evaded, we go back to talking to our Father and King only when we want or need something. We spiritually starve ourselves until we're near death, and when we run out of other options, we binge on God.

Of course, the routine is interrupted when we stumble upon one of the special days or events when it's culturally acceptable to be overly religious, such as Christmas or Easter or when we are getting married or having our first child. In those moments we carefully reengage our Christian vocabulary, and we work hard to appear pious. We get caught up in the rhythm of spiritual activity, but our activity isn't the desire of our soul. It's just activity.

This is a prescription for hypocritical, inauthentic faith. This is how we develop an undernourished, distracted, dishonest soul. If we're really going to have a healthy soul, we need to give consistent time and effort to our relationship with God. Like Jesus, we have to go to quiet places and pray, and we have to make war against the distractions that keep us from God.

Combating the Information Age

Unfortunately, quiet places are becoming difficult to find. I sometimes feel as if I'm living in a gigantic tin can filled with speakers attached to iPods playing dozens of different styles of music at full volume at the same time. This world is full of all kinds of indiscernible noise.

People call this the information age, and I think that's a good name for it. Information is spinning around us. It spins in and out of our ears and minds, through our cell phones, through our computers and our iPods. This is a world teeming with ambient noise. Every moment, we're enduring a 360-degree information assault. Yes, I feel *assaulted* by noise and information. They crowd out my ability to contemplate important things, and sometimes I can barely keep a single train of thought.

I came to a crashing realization of this at work the other day. By ten in the morning, the day already felt long. I had an impossible list of things to do, and my time tank was leaking. Worse yet, every single task on my list was an urgent one. All of them were due yesterday, and I had been in my office running in place for days, making hardly any progress.

Literally—for days. Everything was unfinished and overdue, but that wasn't the problem. I wasn't making any progress despite all my busyness and work. To make it worse, my office was filled with a cacophony of alarms and task-list reminders and phone calls asking

for completed projects and unanswered e-mails of good people wondering what my problem was.

It was major-league chaos, and I was drowning. So, I paused, even
amid all the noise. I didn't have time to waste for a pause, but I was
running out of options. I felt as if I were holding a time bomb, and my
heart was beating out of my chest as I listened to it tick.

I knew I needed a few minutes of rehab before this bomb exploded.
So I put everything down and got quiet. I started thinking about how
I had been managing my time, what I had prioritized, and how I had
worked on pressing matters. I asked myself what was important, what
was *most* important, and why the most important things weren't getting more of my attention.

Then I diagnosed a stunningly simple problem that was nearly crippling my productivity. Every day, while I worked, I kept my inbox
open on my computer screen. Each new e-mail, buzz of my Blackberry,
or ding on my Mac was another distraction banging on the door of my
mind. I would get one step ahead on a project just to be thrown two
steps behind by offering a "quick" answer to a new e-mail.

My "quick" answers had become bombs that exploded my train of
thought on whatever else I was working on. My inbox was trying to kill
me, and I was letting it! I was letting my own personal serial killer have
its way with me. How on earth could I finish some difficult task with
this clicking and clanging and banging on the door of my mind every
few minutes? I had become like a kid trying hard to do his homework
with a hair band screaming in the background!

I'm convinced that having a consistent relationship with God is
much more difficult in the information age than it was before. Living
honestly—living what we believe—is difficult in an environment that's
always buzzing and blinking and ringing with technology. And nearly
everyone has been diagnosed with some kind of attention-deficit disorder, so we have convinced ourselves that we are incapable of winning
our war with distraction.

I took one of those ADHD tests online. I did great. I scored off
the charts. It was one of the highest grades I'd ever earned. I was kind
of proud of myself. But I don't think my high score was the result of a

genetic disorder. Rather, our culture has nearly drowned me in a perpetual waterfall of information, so thinking straight for more than 35 seconds is becoming harder and harder.

In fact, sometimes I feel as if running a triathlon would be easier than getting a little quiet. Nurturing my soul is just plain hard in the information age—like doing a backstroke through sludge—and I'm convinced that one of the greatest challenges to my faith is to figure out how to manage the distractions.

The self-help gurus are right when they tell us we can't do anything well if we're doing everything. Sometimes we have to press the pause button on less important things so we can do what's most important. We don't press that button too often because we've been trained to love our daily swim through the information sewer.

In fact, I actually think we're addicted to it. We might think we're digital superheroes who can juggle ten thousand tasks and still have enough energy left over to live life well. But we're not! Or if we are superheroes, we're bad ones, getting life served in our faces by the clicking and beeping of inanimate objects.

Getting *How* Between *I Should* and *I Will*

Jesus modeled focused, prayerful rest. He also gave us some good advice to follow, and that 2000-year-old advice is especially helpful in the information age. Like most of Jesus' teaching, it's fairly easy to understand. He said, "But when you pray, go into your room and shut the door and pray to your Father" (Matthew 6:6 ESV).

When I first read this potent little verse, I noticed two things. First, Jesus says, "When you pray." Do you see what I see? He doesn't say, "*If* you pray." No, he says, "When you pray." He's assuming that if you're serious about your spiritual life, you are a praying person. Let's just get this one nailed down. People who follow Jesus, people who nourish their souls, are people who shut off the distractions and dedicate time and energy to prayer. It's not a matter of *if*, it's a matter of *when*. So I guess the first decision we need to make is when are we going to pray.

The second phrase floored me too. "Go into your room and shut the door." It's not really difficult either. Jesus says you have to shut the door. Just shut the door to the world. Today he would probably mean shutting the door to text messages and e-mails, phone calls, multitasking, and our 50 other kinds of distractions.

This makes perfect sense because prayer is sacred, and it's important enough to put everything else on hold for a few minutes. After all, if you were having a private meeting with the president of the United States, would you leave him waiting while you responded to a text message? Of course not! We should have the same solemnity in our appointments with God.

Some early rabbis used some extreme statements to teach their pupils about the sacredness and importance of prayer. "Even if a king were to greet you or if a snake curls at your feet, never stop praying!"[1] Today those rabbis would say, "Even if your cell phone rings twice, you get twelve text messages, five Facebook friend requests, and forty-four e-mails, don't stop praying!"

Here's a 2000-year-old tip from Jesus: You have to shut the door and keep it shut. Linger there. Study, think, pray. No multitasking! Multitasking is like the Ebola virus to your soul.

If you want to know who God is, start by pressing the pause button in your life. You have to pause from everything else, and you have to communicate with God—alone. You talk to him through prayer as he communicates to you through the Bible, through the Holy Spirit, through your circumstances, and through other believers.

And in addition to pressing the pause button, you also have to develop some kind of growth plan so you'll know what to do when you pause.

It's like Going to the Gym

The apostle Paul told the members of his favorite church, "Work out your salvation with fear and trembling." I know some people who started to work out. After a while, muscles started popping out of nowhere, fat started fading away, and energy and adrenaline started pumping through their veins. People who work out inevitably get stronger, leaner, and more energetic.

And the more you work out, the stronger you get. The change isn't immediately apparent, but it's happening. You don't morph from science-book nerd to Mr. World overnight. It takes time.

It also takes consistency.

But after a little time and consistency, people start to notice a difference. You run into girls or guys who turned you down in high school, and they stutter and stammer as they look at the new you and ask, "What happened to you?"

"Oh, been working out."

"Wow! Well, maybe we can get coffee sometime."

You remember when they rejected you, and you know this is your moment for revenge. So you reply, "Well…I'm kind of busy." Then you turn and walk away with a little, proud smile on your face because revenge is sweet. It's not Jesus-like, but it's sweet!

An effective workout also requires the right regimen. You pick the right machines and weights, and you do the right amount of reps on the right days. The more you do, the stronger you get. You never change automatically; you get to your goal one rep at a time. Similarly, you grow spiritually strong one step at a time, one day at a time, and one prayer at a time.

People think they will become spiritually mature by some act of God, as if they didn't have to put in any work. Sorry—nothing works this way. Athletes don't become strong without work, businessmen don't become successful without work, and a politician doesn't become president unless he runs a good campaign. Even melodramatic celebrities are consistently losing and gaining weight and learning hundreds of lines before their movies.

Why do we think God is just going to sprinkle magic holy water on us to make us spiritually healthy? He didn't design the universe this way. The universe is a place of cause and effect, and we largely get out of things what we put into them. God is at work helping you grow spiritually, but the same rule generally applies. Sometimes you get out of your spiritual life what you put into it.

A Workout Plan

Now, I don't go to a real gym very often. You'd know it if you saw me. I'm small. I have *zero* muscles. I normally only go to a real gym after Thanksgiving or when I've binged on fried chicken.

So do you know what my major problem is when I go to a real gym? I have no idea what to do. The machines look to me like medieval torture devices. I don't know how to use them or what they're for, and the gym's clientele scares me to death. Some people in our local gym have forearms the size of my thighs. Doing curls with an eight-pound dumbbell next to some grunting Cyclops who bench-presses his car every Tuesday can be kind of intimidating.

I imagine sometimes people feel this way about their faith. First, it's kind of intimidating to be a beginning believer, especially if you should have been getting strong a long time ago. But this challenge of intimidation is just an illusion. All people struggle and strain in the gym, whether they lift 8 pounds or 800, and all Christians struggle to grow strong at times. You need not feel intimidated when you step into the spiritual gym. Instead, you can feel proud for deciding to do something good for yourself.

As for understanding what to do once you get there, I can help you with this one. You can consider me your personal spiritual trainer, and these five steps are your workout plan. This is your regimen. Do this when you press the pause button.

1. *Pray.* Stop first and pray to God. You don't have to worry about using Elizabethan English. In fact, don't. Just talk to God the way you'd talk to me. Begin by thanking him for the good things in your life and praising him for the good things he's done, and then ask any requests you have. Finally, end by asking him to speak to you as you study his Word.

2. *Read.* Digest a verse or a chapter in the Bible every time you sneak away to pray. There is no rule—just read something. Maybe read the chapter in Proverbs that corresponds with the day of the month (Proverbs has 31 chapters), a couple of verses in one of the Gospels, or a psalm. This is about quality more than quantity, so reading

half of a verse carefully is better than laboring through four chapters mindlessly.

3. *Think*. After you read, pause and think about what you read. Maybe ask yourself some questions, or go online and look up what you don't understand. (When you do, don't open your e-mail!) It's desperately important that you pause to think, to meditate, and to contemplate what you're reading, or you'll never understand it.

4. *Write*. This step helps you think better. Find a small journal and make a few notes on what you read. Write down things you found interesting, questions you might have, or lessons you learned. Something about writing causes you to comprehend what's going on in your mind. I'm not talking about keeping a diary; rather, simply move truth from your head to your hands. It doesn't have to be organized, grammatically correct, or exhaustive. Just write or scribble something.

5. *Do*. Finally, and most importantly, ask yourself if there's a way you can do what you read about. Ask yourself how this truth applies to your life or to the life of others. This is the step where you start to live differently. If you never apply this step, you'll never change, and you'll never become spiritually healthier. And you'll never live what you believe.

I don't gamble because I'm not a very lucky guy, but I would be willing to bet if you press pause and apply these five steps for a few minutes a couple times this week, you will start noticing positive change in your life.

There are two images you might have in your head as you approach this new discipline. The first is of people walking into their workout with their head down in embarrassment and shame because they have neglected their health and don't know what to do. The second image is of people walking into the building with their head high, accompanied by the standing ovation of a cheering crowd.

The second image is the right one for you.

Imagine for a minute that you are a professional football player running for the game-winning touchdown as thousands of fans bellow their loudest cheers. Can you hear that noise? Can you feel the rumble of that stadium? Don't you feel as if their voices are blowing you forward? That's the image I'm encouraging you to have. You may not think you can make it to the spiritual end zone, but I know you can. I've seen a lot of rookies make *big* plays.

Christians from generations before believe you can. And Jesus will put the wind behind your back.

The first step to the end zone happens in the training room. It's a step out of the noise and into the quiet. Why not do it now?

Then *run!*

GIVING IN TO THE WILL OF GOD
THE REBELLIOUS SOUL

8

O kay, so now we're in the gym, we have a workout plan, and we know where we're going: We want to live honest, authentic, committed lives of faith. We want to live what we believe.

In the last chapter, I suggested that you pray, read, think, write, and do. But there's a problem. Many times we never get to the doing, and it's in the doing of our faith that things start to change. Only when we *do* what we know we should do will we start to honestly live what we say we believe. That's simple enough, right? This is kindergarten theology. Do what God tells you to do. It's not enough to just believe. Those who don't live what they believe are hypocrites. None of us like hypocrites.

The doing is the water sprayed onto the blooming flowers by a caring gardener. It is the salt added to bland food. It's the remodeling of an old house. It's the difference between a hypocrite and an authentic believer. It's when belief conceives.

And it's a matter of spiritual life or death. All the spiritual passion and activity we can muster will be totally useless if we never decide to submit to that truth and actually practice it in our daily lives. If truth never makes it to our hands and our feet, our mouths and our minds, we are like a person who has architectural drawings for a dream house and the money to build it but never actually builds the house.

And there is one fantastic challenge awaiting you when you start the doing. Doing what God says often calls for a battle of wills. Your will must ultimately be subservient to his will for your life. A healthy spiritual life requires more than daily time with God. It also requires daily submission of our wills to him in the living out of our faith.

Submitting Our Individualism to God

For me, this is a daily struggle. Sometimes it's just plain hard to submit my will to God and to do what he says is best instead of what I think is best. This is especially difficult for me because of my personality. I've always had a type A attitude about life. Right now, for instance, I'm on my way to Mexico for a few days of vacation with my wife. She is sleeping on my left side. She's not the only one. Almost everyone on this airplane is sleeping.

I am awake. As usual, I've decided to take advantage of a little extra time to get caught up on some work instead of grabbing a little nap. Why? Because I'm a type A kind of guy. It's always been this way.

Sometimes being type A is a blessing. Sometimes it's a curse. Sometimes it's funny. One day when I was nine years old, my dad took me to work with him. Of course, I wasn't content to just sit in a chair and play video games next to my dad all day. No, I wanted a piece of the action, and because Dad was a manager, I knew no one could do anything about it. So I decided it was my turn to call the shots.

I showed up to work dressed in a suit and a clip-on tie, and all day I marched around the office as if I were the boss. I paraded from one end of the car dealership to the other, "supervising" things. I held my head high and put my shoulders back, and if I saw a customer whom no one had noticed, I rustled up one of my dad's employees from his coffee break and forced him to latch onto the unsuspecting shopper. I was dead serious about my responsibility. One time I walked one of my dad's employees to a customer, all the while scolding him for neglecting to pay attention to the arrival of new customers. I patronized him like I was a 50-year-old executive. "I should never have to do this for you. This is *your* job, not my job!"

Dad's employees hated me. They referred to me as the Nazi and Attila the Hun and some other nicknames a good Christian boy shouldn't include in a book like this one. Sometimes people think it's cute when the boss' adorable little kid comes to work with him. Not these guys. They dreaded me like the plague. They would rather have Dad bring a starved grizzly bear to the office than little Johnnie.

It has always been this way. In sixth grade I decided we needed a school newspaper, so naturally, I started one. I persuaded my teacher, the principal, and the other teachers to let me create the newspaper. They were worried about the time and resources it would consume.

I said, "Don't worry about it; I'll take care of it." And, somehow, I did take care of it. I immediately went to work recruiting the writers and putting the different parts of the newspaper together. Within a couple of months, we had produced the inaugural edition of *Cat Scratch Fever* and sold enough copies to finance a month of field trips at the end of the semester. If I wasn't busy enough creating, editing, typesetting, designing, and publishing the newspaper, I decided I would also like to write an undercover advice column. So I did it. I wrote under the moniker *Motormouth*, and when no one sent me questions, I created my own. I wrote with all my heart and dished out all the advice a sixth grader could muster!

Almost from infancy I have been an aggressive, impetuous, and get-it-done type of guy. I want to call the shots, I want to make the rules, I want to be the master of my own destiny. I don't like submitting to other people's control and authority. I like being an independent, free-thinking, unaccountable individual. I am inclined to do what's best for me in all situations, and I feel entitled to.

If you're an American, you probably have some of this in your personality. Most Americans are fiercely individualistic and independent. We are taught from birth to watch our own backs and to achieve our own dreams. We are told that we can do anything if we just put our minds to it. We are not a collectivistic society, glued together by our communities. We are entrenched in our individualism. We often say it's our way or the highway.

In fact, Americans almost worship their individualism and their freedom. We feel entitled to our rights. We can't even order our food off of a standard menu—we have to customize it for our own tastes, and we feel entitled to have it our way.

The problem is that if we are to live lives that are pleasing to God, we can't have it our own way. The very first effect of living our beliefs is that we begin to put God on the throne of our lives, and we take an inferior place. We have to let him be in charge; otherwise, we are assuming his position as Lord of our lives.

No More Idols

All of this individualism runs deep and is pervasive. It's also almost indistinguishable from idolatry.

Idolatry is sometimes called the root of all sin—for good reason. It is essentially making war against God. Idolaters prioritize other things, other persons, other preferences, or even themselves above God. When we do that, we might as well build our own golden calf and start wandering through the desert, just as the children of Israel did. That's what idolatry does to us. It lands us in a wasteland where we slowly die of spiritual dehydration. Even worse, it's completely unnecessary—the living water we need for life is always available to us.

The problem with idolatry is that idol worshippers settle for a cheap substitute of the real thing. This is what frustrated the prophets in the Old Testament more than anything else. When you read their rants against the worship of statutes, you sense they are completely exasperated, saying in effect, "Why don't you go talk to your idol!"

Can you hear the sarcasm? The prophet is saying, "The idol has a mouth, but it can't talk. It has eyes, but it can't see. You worship it, but you made it with your own hands. This just doesn't make any sense!"

Of course, most of us aren't bowing down to little statues. Our idols are more sinister. They are usually intangible, almost invisible, but equally destructive. Our idols are probably more dangerous than handmade relics, and they are just as unable to satisfy our desperate need for God.

This is especially true when we turn ourselves into idols. Every time we let our wills triumph over God's will, we're nominating ourselves as the gods of our lives. Eventually, we'll remember that we are utterly unable to meet our own needs and fix our own problems and find ultimate meaning in our lives. This realization might come after a season of grasping for money or relationships, notoriety or popularity, celebrity or success. In the end, if we achieve fame and fortune, we will also find those pursuits to be insufficient to quiet the longings we have inside of us. Any idol is an insufficient substitute for an omnipotent and loving God who talks, who listens, and who is active in the world and in the universe.

Our idols are those things we value above God, and they reveal our relationship with the truth. They are the things we think we can't live without. They include beliefs that conflict with the beliefs established by God. They are not necessarily bad; they are just misplaced.

Stop. Slow down for one second. Ask yourself this question: Do you value anything above God? Even yourself?

Idolatry is a nuclear bomb to your spiritual life because it knocks out the main thing first. When we idolize something above God, we can't get past Moses' first commandment: "You shall have no other gods before me."[1] We begin by losing.

Regardless of how hard we try to look good and to live in a way that makes us seem Christian, we will remain stuck at square one. We are following our own truth and not God's truth. If I don't address my idolatry, all my religious activity—reading my Bible and going to church and trying to do the right things—won't accomplish much. I'm like a kid trying to do trigonometry before mastering arithmetic.

I have to regularly identify those things in my life that subvert God's influence, and I have to intentionally overcome them with the intensity of a soldier restraining insurgents. I have to decide that God alone will remain on the throne of my life. As I come to God, I recognize that I'm coming to the source of truth. What is true *for me* is not what matters; he *is* the truth, and I have to admit that his way really is the best way.

The Lie That Leads to Rebellion

One of the enemy's first lies in the garden continues to be his greatest: "God is keeping something good from you." This thinking taunts us to believe that some tremendous pleasure or joy is hiding on the other side of a prohibition. We refer to this shared human experience as "eating forbidden fruit." The ancient lie is part of the enemy's clandestine plan to convince us to unseat God again and to exchange our version of truth for his truth, our will for his will.

The serpent in the Garden of Eden convinced Adam and Eve to eat the fruit of the tree of the knowledge of good and evil by telling them that it would somehow make them like God. He convinced them that God was keeping something enjoyable from them and that they could be the masters of their own destiny. The deceiver was trying to paint God as deceptive. God had warned Adam and Eve about the consequences for awakening sin in the world.

When Adam and Eve chose to eat the forbidden fruit, they chose their will instead of God's will, their desire instead of God's desire, and the path to death rather than life. The world is still reeling from the consequences of that single decision.

We make similar decisions today, and they always lead to a death of some sort. The enemy doesn't have new ideas. He has engaged in the same vicious tactic since the beginning of human history. He tries to deceive us into thinking that God's ways are not the best ways, and he tells us that there is more to life than God wants us to realize.

This tactic triggers our individualism gone wild, and we suddenly find ourselves turning away from the voice of God. In the end, we idolize something that will eventually kill us if we let it.

A Daily Fight

This is why Jesus said to love the Lord our God with all of our heart. He used the word *heart* to refer to our will. In our will, we decide what we will believe and how we will live. We can ask ourselves, how would God like me to make this decision? What would God like for me to do today with my life, with my money, with my relationship, with my time? Is what I'm doing pleasing to God?

Jesus knew this would be a daily battle for us, so he told us to pray regularly, "Your kingdom come, your will be done." Why did he include this in his prayer? Jesus knew that from the very beginning, man has had a tendency to let his own will trump God's will. So he advised us to ask God to help us embrace his will and his kingdom, to submit to God's desire over our own desire, every day. He knew we would have to fight daily to keep ourselves from climbing onto God's throne again because the same serpent's voice encourages us to ignore God, to eat forbidden fruit, to believe his lies.

When Jesus taught this, he knew our propensity to prioritize our will over God's will, and he also knew the consequences of rebelling against God, his will, and his truth. In John 10:10, Jesus said, "The thief comes only to steal and kill and destroy; I have come that they might have life, and have it to the full." According to Jesus, we can submit to God's truth, which leads to life, or we can follow the lies of the deceiver, which lead to robbery, death, and destruction.

It's a daily battle, and it's a matter of life or death.

So in order to shield ourselves from the destructive lies of the enemy, we must appreciate that God is the source of real truth, we must devote ourselves to this truth, and we must turn from the idols in our lives that would exalt themselves and turn us away from God and his truth. Otherwise, we're choosing to live in a spiritual desert instead of an oasis that is lush with God's living water.

PART 3

FROM A HEALTHY SOUL TO PERSEVERANCE

F aith says, "I trust God, regardless of what is happening. I will press on; I will not be a wishy-washy, halfhearted, fair-weather friend of God. I will trust God when it's difficult. I will persevere when I see the night is coming. I will persevere when life is hard, when I fail, and when I don't feel like persevering."

If I believe in God and I have accepted his truth, I know that he will guard my life. So I will choose to trust him every step of the way.

WE ARE "GET BACK UP AGAIN" PEOPLE
WHAT TO DO WHEN YOU FAIL

9

My wife and I invited some American and Brazilian friends to our home to watch America's opening game in the World Cup. We worked all day to get the house ready and prepare a smorgasbord of snacks. I even decided to prepare my inaugural batch of chocolate chip cookies.

Then the bottom fell out. An enormous thunderstorm rolled onto the horizon. The clouds approached menacingly as we stared out the window, and within minutes the wind and rain started pummeling our house. The raindrops slammed against the ground, and a vicious wind churned the calm outside into pure meteorological chaos. The miniature hurricane came from nowhere and made a royal mess of our afternoon. Any minute I expected a car to go flying by our window.

We watched a flowerpot crash to the ground with a gust of wind. The lights flickered. And then the cable went out. All of this just about the time I realized the cookies were still in the oven.

We had guests arriving momentarily to watch an all-important soccer game, but we had no television, a broken flowerpot on our front porch, and a plateful of burned chocolate chip cookies. I ate about five charred cookies in rapid succession (trying to prove to myself they were actually edible).

We tried to plaster polite smiles on our faces as we watched our friends trudge into our newly cleaned sitting room with their rainy shoes. It was a disaster. I sat down in exasperation and wondered, "Is God picking on us?"

No, it was just a bad day. We all have bad days.

Christianity Isn't a Peace Treaty with Life

Let's correct a common misperception. Deciding to pursue a healthy relationship with God—to live honestly, to live what you believe—is not a way of bribing God to make your life easy. You will still have bad days. Whether you're the world's most faithful Christian or God's most ardent enemy, things will be difficult sometimes. God teaches us in Scripture that the pain and trouble of life is the product of the fall of man. It is the ultimate result of sin being set loose in the world, and it's just the natural outplaying of life on earth. God isn't sitting at a set of cosmic dials, determining whom he's going to harass today. Rather, sin is like a mad bull running through the china shop of your serenity, making a mess of things every chance it gets.

Deciding to pursue a deeper relationship with God will not shield you from life's painful and difficult seasons. But God will help you interpret those difficulties properly, he will provide you with the resolve to make it through when things get hard, and he will empower you to overcome—to be more than a conqueror.[1]

Still, everyone has difficulties in life. It's useless to try to avoid your inevitable encounters with life's problems. You'll be much better off learning how to deal with them. Even the best Christians will get beat up by life sometimes. Whether we get clobbered by things that are out of our control or we end up facedown in wreckage of our making, the question is not *if* things will go bad for us. It's a matter of *when*.

When, Not If

If you don't believe me, just look a couple people in the eye and ask, "How are you, really?" That simple question can get you in a lot of trouble. You might open a Pandora's box stuffed with junk. People might look tidy on the outside, but inside their lives might look like the Beverly Hillbillies' truck loaded down with a houseful of baggage.

You might be assaulted with a vivid description of every possible ache and pain imaginable. You could hear about Uncle Bill's accident or some guy's best friend's brother, whose girlfriend just dropped him, or Aunt Ethel's "condition." As people moan on and on, you might begin to regret even caring to ask. You'll be dodging the fallout of a well-intentioned question because these people perceive their glass as half empty. Everything is always bad, and every new challenge is just one more chapter in the story of how God is picking on them. They believe that another piece of bad news is lurking under every unturned stone. Every problem, big or small, leads to another crisis.

The truth is, things are difficult for all of us sometimes, and this is exactly why we shouldn't exaggerate our small problems. We will eventually have big problems. We will all cry our share of tears after midnight news shakes our peaceful worlds. We will all have our financial challenges and our relational struggles, and all of us will at some point exhaust our options.

We will fail. We will stumble.

Even as well-intentioned Christians, we will sometimes respond to these troubles in ways that only make matters worse. We will disappoint ourselves, and we will disappoint others because we are deeply flawed people who are apt to prove it by our decisions.

Therefore, since life is full of surprises, we should be prepared for the threat of failure and discouragement at any time. Regardless of who you are, how much money you have, and how peaceful and secure your life might seem to be, you will have to learn how to cope with life's surprises.

You could have the faith of Moses, Paul, and David all rolled up in one and still deal with failure and discouragement. Like Moses, you will one day strike a rock in frustration, or you will fight like Paul with your own thorn in the flesh, or you will find your Goliath-defeating courage insufficient in war with your own demons. But some people (like Moses, Paul, and David) have learned to bounce back when life throws them down. They are the ones who are able to do the most and be the most for God.

Here's the secret you need to navigate life's failures and frustration: Half the battle in life isn't dealing with our problems, but handling our perception of our problems. Remember that age-old adage, "perception is reality"? In actuality, it often is.

For example, do you remember the last time your alarm didn't go off in the morning? When you finally opened your eyes and stared in total disbelief at the clock, you were faced with the reality that you were going to be late for school or work again. What was your immediate thought? "It's going to be a terrible day!" Right? You immediately resign yourself to a full day of failure! And your day may well have turned out to be terrible because perceptions are powerful, and when left to their own, they have a way of becoming self-fulfilling prophecies.

On days like that, I'll drag myself out of the house, stumble through my duties, and think the entire time, "Everything will go downhill from here." Soon my expectation of a bad day will have sabotaged any hope that things might turn around for good. Why? Perceptions are powerful.

Frederick the Great and His Potatoes

Frederick the Great, the eighteenth-century king of Prussia, learned a lot about the power of our perceptions when he decided to introduce the potato into the diet of his subjects. He quickly learned that perception could be the enemy *or* the friend of progress.

Prussia depended heavily on bread, and the king realized the potato could provide another staple and protect the kingdom against famine. It could also shield his people from the price instability connected to bread. Frederick reasoned that if he could just introduce the potato into the regular diets of his subjects, he could help solve both problems at once.

Unfortunately, his simple idea was foiled by his subjects' perception of potatoes! People in Prussia hadn't thought of potatoes as food. The crop was ugly—it was brown and speckled with outgrowths. It grew in the ground, and it was hard and relatively tasteless. It was also not native to Europe. Potatoes arrived on ships from South America, and the Prussians were prejudiced against their colonial neighbors in the southern hemisphere. If potatoes were useful for anything, they were food for animals or the worst kind of paupers, but they were not to be consumed by respectable people.

But King Frederick was committed to changing this perception for the sake of his kingdom. So he issued an order in 1774 demanding the growth and consumption of potatoes. His edict was wildly unpopular. In fact, the citizens of one city called Kolberg replied to their king with some quite grumpy words: "The things have neither smell nor taste; not even the dogs will eat them, so what use are they to us?"

So Frederick, who wouldn't accept failure, went back to the drawing board and formulated a more tactical strategy to change the populace's negative perception of potatoes. Long before the introduction of contemporary psychology, the king pulled from his arsenal a little reverse psychology. Frederick would wield a psychological weapon in his fight to change the perception of potatoes for the good of his people.

As the story (or legend!) goes, within days of revoking his previous order, the king ordered the planting of a royal field of potatoes just outside his own palace. He decided to overcome the ramshackle reputation of the potato by rebranding it as royal food. He had potatoes at his own palace, and when he spoke of the rejected vegetable, he spoke of it as food only befitting of a royal.

Then, brilliantly, he stationed a heavy guard around his royal potato field to intimidate potential thieves. Yet these potato police were given rather peculiar instructions. They were to appear legitimate but to turn a blind eye to all thieves! The wise king knew that the neighboring peasants would be tempted to steal anything guarded so heavily.

Within weeks, the theft began.

Eventually, the successful thieves talked to one another, sharing their newfound pathways into the gardens, and soon the stolen potatoes began to be grown, shared, and distributed among the lower class. The king's potatoes had found their way into dozens of peasant gardens. He had purposely created a black market! Simultaneously, the Prussian elites, in their ever-present attempt to maintain their social status, began following the new potato craze.

Call it sinister or call it brilliant, but it worked. King Frederick eventually changed the perception of the potato, and with this tectonic shift of perception he was able to solve a huge societal problem. If he hadn't persevered in his goal of changing the perception of potatoes, they might have never been integrated into the Prussian diet, and perhaps many people would have eventually suffered.

Learning to Perceive a Crisis Differently

Our biggest problems are not necessarily our most apparent problems. Our perceptions of those problems often get us in more trouble than the problems themselves. What if we started perceiving many of our challenges differently? What if we chose to believe that God was actually up to something in our lives even when things seemed dreary and hopeless and painful? After all, certain uneasy seasons of life might eventually turn out to be our misunderstood potatoes.

My parents' divorce and all the accompanying insanity nearly killed my relationship with God. It also killed my sense of security and stability, and it put enough wounds on my heart to employ a personal shrink for a lifetime.

My family was suddenly thrust into poverty (in the American sense of the word), and I had to live with the haunting memory of my suicidal dad limp in the seat of his car. We moved from house to house and school to school so many times that I hardly have any social roots from my childhood. My family was written off and avoided by the church. We were scorned, shamed, and embarrassed. It was hard—very, very hard.

Worse yet, all of this happened just after I decided to care about my spiritual health, just after I became convinced of Jesus as my Savior, just after I chose to have a daily meeting with God from nine to nine thirty every night.

It was all bad, right? I could ask myself, "Why did Jesus put me through all of this just when I decided to get serious about serving him?" I could decide that God must have been picking on me, and slowly that attitude would turn toward resentment. Eventually I would move away from the very thing I need in my life the most—God.

Or I can try to interpret my circumstances with an attitude of trust in a God whose ways are higher than my ways. I can choose to see my life through a lens of grace, and I can choose to believe that God might be up to something.

Today, when I look back on my parents' divorce, I perceive things differently than I did before. I can see that God was with us every step of the way. We were in poverty, but we were never homeless. The church might have misunderstood us, but a few people in the church were always ready to seek us out and care for us. We all survived our relational war despite the perilous moments!

My testimony confirms what one man said: "God never puts more on us than he puts in us." Charles Spurgeon, the great British pastor, once said, "God is too good to be unkind, too wise to be mistaken, and when I cannot trace His hand, I can always trust His heart." In hindsight, now I realize the effects of my parents' divorce were not nearly as detrimental as they might have been.

When we start to perceive our circumstances in a hopeful light, grace begins to peek through the darkness of our difficult days. We start to realize that God wasn't waiting in the wings. He was involved. At times his involvement might have seemed clandestine, but we have no idea how God has manipulated history on our behalf. Sometimes he has intervened in ways we'll never know, and his silence in our crisis may be the best gift he could possibly give us.

Today, I feel nearly healed, and God is using my story to encourage thousands of people to run toward God in their troubles and not away from him. I also see God at work healing my family. I can see so clearly how he has always been looking out for us. Life is better because of all the lessons I learned during that difficult season, and I have deeper faith in God because of the way he helped me.

A couple of years ago I overcame my relational anxiety and met the woman of my dreams. We just celebrated our one-year anniversary. And today, I'm not weighed down by the baggage of my childhood. I have a good career as one of North America's youngest university executives, and God is using his work of grace in my life as a testimony to encourage a lot of other hurting people. And I'm not the only one God has redeemed. My mom just remarried, and my dad is one of my best friends. My dad even listens to my sermons online each week.

God did not cause my parents' marriage to fall apart. They did. God was not complicit in their sin and their failure, but he was and is complicit in their healing. He is a God who mends our brokenness and turns our stories of failure, discouragement, and pain into testimonies of grace and perseverance.

With God, I have learned that there is a light at the end of every tunnel. He is always keeping watch over us when life is trying to beat us down, and so many times he intervenes before things become critical. He doesn't have to intervene, but he chooses to because he loves us more than we'll ever know.

Why God Lets Life Be Hard Sometimes

You might still wonder why Jesus would let me endure all of this just when I decided to get serious about serving him. The best way I can answer this question is by introducing you to a story.

My friend Dwayne is a great father. He has four children—two girls and two boys. Dwayne was rough around the edges in high school. He was a cultural Christian who partied hard and didn't care much about God. But then God went after him.

Dwayne became a believer, left his former life, and decided to become a pastor. He's been a pastor for 27 years now, and he's a genuinely good and godly man. He's the kind of dad who takes his daughters on their first date, who teaches his kids the Bible over dinner, and who models what he believes. He's not a hypocrite. He loves God and his family deeply, and he's obsessed with helping others to find the most in their relationship with Jesus. He coaches his son's football and baseball teams, and he takes his kids to his father's farm to teach them real-life parables. His kids live what he's taught them.

One of Dwayne's sons is a good football player, and Dwayne's a proud daddy. He's also his son's coach. During one game, his son was pretty beaten up. He was dazed and wounded with a bloody and painful injury, and he was exhausted. His son wanted to quit, but Dwayne believed he had more fight left in him. Dwayne had a decision to make as a coach and as a father.

His son's injury wasn't critical. The boy was one of the best players on the team, and the score was tight. It could go either way. Dwayne needed his son to play despite his injury, and he didn't want his son to learn to quit when things were hard.

Dwayne loved his son as much as a father could love a son, and I'm sure he was tempted to let him sit on the bench, take a rest, and get himself back together. But because he loved his son, he knew him well enough to know actually how bad he was hurt and what else he could handle. I'm pretty sure Dwayne believed in his son more than the boy believed in himself. So Dwayne pulled the little guy to his side, grabbed him by his facemask, and encouraged him to get back into the game.

Though Dwayne's son was beaten up, bloodied, and in pain, Dwayne knew his son could do it. He knew he had more fight in him. As a good dad and as a good coach, he had two goals in mind. First, he wanted his son to learn that he could do more than he believed he could, and second, he didn't want to rob the team of the contribution of one of its best players.

The other day I was talking to Dwayne about this scenario, and I asked him why he made this decision. Dwayne said, "I didn't want him to learn to quit when he wanted to. I knew if he learned to quit this early in life, he would be tempted to give up any time things got hard. He doesn't realize yet how hard life is. I know how hard life is. As a dad who cares about his son, I know he needs to learn to play hurt, and I believed he could do it."

I think this is also why God throws us into the game sometimes when we think we can't handle it. He is teaching lessons we can learn only in the fight. He is galvanizing our faith and showing us things about him as our coach. He aims to teach us lessons we wouldn't otherwise know, lessons we can only learn on the field.

God sometimes allows us to encounter pain and doubt and difficulty, and he sometimes forces us to play hurt because he believes in us more than we believe in ourselves and sees in us more than we see in ourselves. It's one of his ways of teaching us life's most important lessons and of reminding us of his role as our coach.

Every once in a while, life's storms will knock us down. When they do, we can get back up, dust ourselves off, and try again. In the meantime, our Savior, our coach, will always be there, looking out for us and giving us the strength to get back in.

And when we fail (and we will), we must remember that a single failure is not a prophecy of future failures. When we find ourselves stumbling in our relationship with God, disappointed in our decisions, or on the other end of a difficult season of life, we shouldn't stay down long. Christians are "get back up again" people. They have perseverance. They are in the game till the last minute.

The other day, I looked up some famous failures, and I learned some really interesting things.

- Abraham Lincoln failed in business on two occasions, he was defeated in eight political races, he struggled with the death of his fiancée, and he had a nervous breakdown. All of this was before he became president at age 51.

- The Beatles were turned down by recording company executives who determined that guitar music was on the way out.

- Ulysses S. Grant was a failed soldier, farmer, and real estate agent by his thirties.

- Lucille Ball was dismissed from drama school because she was too shy.

- Michael Jordan was cut from his high school basketball team and cried all afternoon.

- A teacher told Thomas Edison he was too stupid to succeed at anything.

- Walt Disney was fired from a newspaper because he lacked imagination and had no original ideas.

Eventually, we must decide to trust God when we have to play hurt, and in the end, we'll probably be stronger. Christians aren't the kind of people who give up easily. Christians are the kind of people that tough it out, get back up again, and play hurt.

Paul said in his letter to the church in Corinth, "We are hard pressed on every side, but not crushed; perplexed, but not in despair; persecuted, but not abandoned; struck down, but not destroyed."[2] The author of Hebrews wrote, "Therefore lift your drooping hands and strengthen your weak knees, and make straight paths for your feet, so that what is lame may not be put out of joint but rather be healed."[3] About a thousand years earlier, David wrote, "A thousand may fall at your side, ten thousand at your right hand, but it will not come near you…if you make the Most High your dwelling…then no harm will befall you, no disaster will come near your tent. For he will command his angels concerning you to guard you in all your ways."[4]

We aren't defined by our failures, but by what we do with them. One of my mentors used to encourage me by saying, "You don't measure a man by his wealth or his talent as the world does, but rather by what it takes to discourage him."

Christians will have their ups and downs. Life will be just as turbulent and bumpy as it is for non-Christians. The Bible says, "[God] sends rain on the righteous and the unrighteous."[5] Yet we are the people of God. We follow a resurrected Savior, and we get back up when life throws us down.

You might be thinking, "But Johnnie, you don't know my problem." You're right. I don't. I may not be able to empathize or understand, and my encouragement to get back up might look like the oversimplified machinations of a kid who knows little about the real world.

But what is your alternative? Do you trust in yourself more than you trust in God? Do you want to simply lie there in your own pit? Instead, why don't you get back up, dust yourself off, and dare to believe that God might actually be up to something.

WHEN YOUR SHIP WRECKS
WHAT TO DO WITH SEASONS OF SUFFERING

10

Wealthy lawyer Horatio Spafford loved Jesus and was committed to him. He was a Christian and model businessman who lived what he believed in his everyday life. He was the kind of man you would expect God to richly reward for his faithfulness and his generosity. But in the 1870s, things started going badly.

Spafford's four-year-old son lost a battle with scarlet fever just about the same time that the Great Chicago Fire destroyed most of his real-estate investments.

Because of the sudden turmoil brought on by these double tragedies, he decided to take his wife and four daughters on a vacation to England. He knew that the whole family needed some space to recover from the loss of his son and part of his fortune. He booked passage on the *Ville du Havre* to take him and his family to Europe for their much-needed holiday.

Just before the vessel was to depart, Spafford got word of an urgent business matter that needed his immediate attention. Rather than spoil his family's vacation, he opted to send his wife and four daughters ahead on the ship to England while he traveled back to Chicago to take care of business. As soon as the crisis was evaded, he planned to make his way back to the coast and board the next available ship to England.

One week later, while Spafford was in still in Chicago and his wife was in Wales, he received an unusual telegram. The words caused a flood of grief to come over him, even worse than the grief of losing his lifelong investments and his four-year-old son. His wife had sent six simple words: "Saved alone. What shall I do?"

Horatio Spafford must have felt as if his heart stopped beating.

His wife was one of the few survivors of a collision between the *Ville du Havre* and the *Loch Earn*. The *Ville du Havre* sank in only 12 minutes. The ocean crash claimed the lives of their four daughters and 222 others. Mrs. Spafford survived only because her unconscious body somehow landed on a buoyant slab of wood. Her final memory was of a wave washing up over her and overpowering her grip on one of her young daughters.

In a few sweeping events, Spafford had lost all five of his children and much of his fortune. He immediately left for Europe. While en route to Wales, the captain notified him when the ship was near the place where his four daughters had perished. He later recounted the moment.

> I was deeply agitated…but I could not [tell myself] my four little girls [were] buried there at the bottom of the ocean. Involuntarily, I lifted my eyes to heaven. Yes, I am sure they are there—on high—and happier far than if they were still with me. So convinced am I of this that I would not [want], for the whole world, that one of my children should be given back to me.[1]

During this difficult season of Horatio Spafford's life, he wrote the hymn those believers were singing at Bishop Rucyahana's church in Rwanda, "It Is Well with My Soul."

Where to Run in Crisis

There are two kinds of crises. There are the crises that we invite into our lives through our foolhardy decisions, and then there are those crises, like Horatio Spafford's, that are not the result of our negligence, but simply the product of life's circumstances. Through the centuries, some people have wrongly attributed all crises to the judgment of God. These misguided people believed in an unspoken law of retribution in which God makes life difficult for people who do bad things, and they assumed that if things are bad in life for someone, that person obviously needs to repent.

Job, the biblical patriarch of suffering, tried to make sense of his situation. His friends asked him what he had done to deserve such treatment. But we know from Scripture that Job's trial was not the product of sin. In fact, like Horatio Spafford, he was a good servant of God.

When we enter into seasons of suffering, we can either run away from our faith because of doubt and disillusionment, or run to our faith because we are searching for refuge and for answers. Many times we run away when we desperately need to run toward God. Running toward God is an act of perseverance.

If you run away you will blame and resent God for not protecting you or not intervening in history on your behalf. You will get angry because of your unanswered prayers, and you will shake your frustrated fist at the skies.

The problem with running away from God when things get hard is that this is exactly when you need to run to him the most. When you are tempted to run away from him, ask yourself, "Where am I to run to for help?"

I read of an atheist who told a *Time* magazine interviewer, "Organized religion is a crutch for weak-minded people." When I first read this, it deeply offended me, but then I rethought it. Now, I know how I would reply to that atheist: "What is *your* crutch when life gets hard, when you have unanswered questions, when you can't make sense of it all? How is that crutch working out for you?"

I actually think that everyone needs a crutch to help them hobble along during life's most difficult experiences because all people are broken and living in a broken world, and we all desperately need God. The question is, how effective are the alternative crutches?

When a crisis arrives, some people try to distract themselves with unhealthy behaviors. They self-medicate. They might become workaholics, or they might start partying. They might try to dull their pain and suppress their problems with narcotics or sex or money or pride. They make these things their crutches to hold them up when the winds of life threaten to blow them down.

Scripture provides the alternative response. The apostle Peter wrote to a bunch of scattered churches, "Cast all your anxiety on [God] because he cares for you."[2]

If Christianity is what we say it is, then it is at its most powerful when we are at the end of ourselves, when life is hard, when we realize how much we actually *need* God. God knows that sometimes if he just solves our presenting problems, if he just gives us more money or heals our relationships or resurrects our child, we will be apt to go back to our perpetual neglect of him.

Instead, he sometimes chooses to perform a greater miracle in our lives than healing our disease or boosting our bank account or repairing our marriage. That miracle might be the act of empowering us to live on despite our pain or to have faith to know our loved ones are enjoying heaven even more than they enjoyed earth.

Some of God's greatest miracles are not his flashiest, such as when he heals our broken hearts, binds up our wounds, and makes us whole again.

God performed a miracle, a real miracle, by helping Horatio Spafford to live another day with so much loss in his life. God performed a miracle when the Rwandans I mentioned earlier smiled again despite the horrors they had experienced. God's healing of a broken heart sometimes seems more amazing than his parting of the Red Sea.

Desperate moments can somehow solidify our faith—if we choose to run into faith for refuge. Running into faith is like running into a fortress when enemy bullets are flying. Job eventually ran into God's arms after enduring impossible suffering. He caps his painful journey in by saying, "My ears had heard of you, but now my eyes have seen you."[3]

The seasons of life that are most likely to cause us to doubt and question God's goodness can serve, in the end, to somehow solidify our belief. Life's trials move us from secondhand faith to eyewitness faith. They take us again to the Grand Canyon.

Why All the Suffering If God Is Good?

If you're like me, when things get hard, you are tempted to ask why. Doubt rises up again to register a complaint. You ask yourself, "Why would God allow all of this pain and trouble and suffering in the lives of people like Horatio Spafford? Why would he not intervene in his life and in my life when I need him? Why doesn't he answer my prayers for help?"

I've spent a lot of time contemplating this question and reading the arguments and ideas of friends and enemies of Jesus as they dissect this issue. I've found good answers to this intellectual challenge in the writings of apologists and great Christian theologians.

I won't repeat their detailed treatment of the issue here. Instead, I will encourage you to read them for yourself, to go on your own journey. But the short answer is this: God has given man a certain degree of freedom. He's not controlling each step that man takes. He doesn't ordain that I drink two cups of coffee instead of one, or that I sit in this chair instead of the chair across the room. God controls the ultimate end of many parts of life, and he certainly intervenes at certain times for certain reasons. But he also allows people to live with a certain degree of freedom.

This is why evil is in the world. God could not design a man who could choose to love him without giving man the freedom not to. If man has the power to choose, he can make all kinds of good and evil choices, and those choices have built-in consequences. God has designed the universe in a way that man's decisions have influence, and man must decide to follow God or not. God is actively involved in the universe and occasionally intervenes for reasons that are often clear only to him, but God also often lets man do his own thing. Each choice has an effect, and God usually lets those choices play out in history. Somehow, in the end, all of those choices work together in a massive, complicated story that he has designed.

C.S. Lewis, the British atheist-turned-Christian academic and the author of books like The Chronicles of Narnia series, had an interesting perspective on the intersection of man's free will and God's control of the universe. Author Philip Yancey describes Lewis' view:

> God created matter in such a way that we can manipulate it,
> by cutting down trees to build houses and damming rivers

to form reservoirs. God granted such an expanse of human freedom that we can oppress each other, rebel against our Creator, even murder God's own Son…We best imagine the world not as a state governed by a potentate but as a work of art, something like a play, in the process of being created. The playwright allows his characters to affect the play itself, then incorporates all their actions into the final result.[4]

Lewis said, "The scene and the general outline of the story is fixed by the author…[but] certain minor details are left for the actors to improvise."[5] God is as providential as he likes to be in parts of the story, in scenes of my story and of your story. Yet in the end, God writes the final chapter, integrating the consequences of each successive event on the earth.

Lewis' perspective helps us find a balance between the control God exerts over the universe and the freedom he gave man to meddle in God's plans.

William Lane Craig, a great defender of Christianity, has drawn from science to demonstrate how the events of our lives and history are actually individual chords struck in a massive orchestration of the universe, composed by God. He says that "chaos theory" demonstrates the intricate interconnectedness of our world. He believes it is a snapshot of how man's seemingly disconnected circumstances might eventually work together for good or bad in God's greater plan. Chaos theory scientists believe that the smallest changes or "disturbances" can have massive effects on our world's weather or insect populations. For instance, a "butterfly fluttering on a twig in West Africa may set in motion forces that will eventually issue a hurricane over the Atlantic Ocean."[6] Craig says that no one observing that butterfly on that twig would ever imagine that such an insignificant event might have such an intricate and complicated outcome.

This is in part what the Bible means when God says, "As the heavens are higher than the earth, so are my ways higher than your ways," or "In all things God works for the good of those who love him, who have been called according to his purpose."[7] Somehow, God has created such a sensitive world that little events can have massive results. Little decisions can end or start wars; they can solve or exacerbate poverty. Little decisions can cause ships to collide and kill 226 people, including Horatio Stafford's four daughters. Little events are dominoes resulting in events that deeply affect our lives in positive and negative ways.

We don't know all that God is up to in his management of this planet of more than six billion people, but we know that sometimes he intervenes and sometimes he doesn't. But through his Word, we know "his divine power has given us everything we need for life and godliness through our knowledge of him"—for the good and bad of it.[8]

He loves us enough sometimes to intervene and sometimes not to intervene. God could have intervened and healed my parents' marriage. Instead, he let it continue its natural progression. The initial result was a lot of pain and brokenness, but now he is using my story to help thousands. His ways were higher than my ways.

God could have somehow kept Horatio Spafford's wife and daughters from the *Ville du Havre* on that fateful day in 1873. Instead, he let those four girls graduate from earth to enjoy an early arrival in heaven. He knew they would be happy to wait for their reunion in the distraction of golden streets and the Son of God. Meanwhile, God used a potent brew of deep faith and deep pain in the lives of Horatio and Anna Spafford to compose a timeless story and a hymn that would strengthen millions through the years in moments of unquenchable pain.

Horatio Spafford never imagined that one day victims of a Rwandan genocide, whose relatives had suffered a much more gruesome and slow death than Spafford's children, would be singing his hymn for their own healing.

The Christian Belief in Resurrection

Early Christians found consolation in their suffering through the hope offered in Christ's resurrection. Paul wrote to a church in the Grecian city of Corinth that the resurrection was the centerpiece of Christian doctrine.[9] He told the church in Rome that salvation is contingent upon believing that Jesus is Lord and confessing that God raised him from the dead.[10] The truth of Jesus' resurrection was not a nebulous doctrine that was celebrated only on Easter. It permeated Christianity, and early Christians drew hope from its reality during times of suffering and persecution.

Paul wrote in one letter about personally suffering horribly under tremendous pressure. He said the pressure was beyond his ability to endure, and at one point the apostle felt as if he was going to die. Yet in this deadly moment of his life, Paul wrote, "This happened that we might not rely on ourselves but on God, who raises the dead."[11]

There are plenty of historical reasons to believe in the resurrection of Jesus Christ.[12] There are also several *practical* reasons to believe, the chief of which is that the resurrection marks the defeat of man's most crippling enemy. If Jesus can triumph over death, he can triumph over any human challenge we might face in our lives. Should he choose to.

The apostle Paul writes in his first letter to the Corinthians that through the resurrection, "death has been swallowed up in victory." Then he speaks to death: "Where, O death, is your victory? Where, O death, is your sting?"[13]

Life will not always be easy. Pain will arrive uninvited, surprises will come, and we can either run away from God or run into his arms. We must *always* choose to run into his arms. He is our only hope, and he has given us good reasons to trust in him. Sometimes, he intervenes and makes things better. Sometimes, he chooses to let us struggle into our faith and fight to survive. Yet he has already done for us two great things.

First, God has given "everything we need for life"[14] through his promise-filled Word and through the testimony of his work through history. Second, he has defeated our greatest enemy, death. He rolled over our death by the death and resurrection of his Son, and he has granted us new life and guaranteed us that he will never leave, even when we must endure great pain.

Recently, I had the opportunity to spend a day at Liberty University with Joni Eareckson Tada. For her entire adult life, she has been confined to a wheelchair due to a tragic diving accident. She has every reason in the world to wonder why God has given her such a difficult lot in life. Yet she has chosen to trust him despite her pain, and she uses her testimony to help millions of struggling believers around the world. Joni once wrote, "Sometimes God allows what he hates to accomplish what he loves."

I think this is true.

Working out all the details is his job. Our job is to trust. Who knows, you might be like a butterfly sitting on a twig, and your suffering might be the first step in an intricate story that could reshape the world.

PART 4

FROM PERSEVERANCE TO MISSION

God uses people to accomplish his plans for earth. He uses people, despite their doubts and failures and flaws, to do truly fantastic things. This is a part of faith in Christ that most people miss. We have to take God's mission personally and determine that we are responsible to make a difference in the world. The good news is that God is already at work in the world, so he is inviting us to be a part of something he's already doing. His mission is our mission, and fulfilling that mission begins with compassion, it requires hard work, and it produces in us a sacrificial spirit based on the realization that the gospel is worth our all.

GOING PUBLIC
BECOMING VOCAL
EYEWITNESSES

Imagine Jesus walking into the room right where you are at this very moment. You are just minding your own business, casually reading this book in a nice comfortable chair on a rainy morning. You're sipping your coffee, you're lost in your imagination, and then, *boom*, Jesus just shows up!

The door creaks a little bit when he walks in. It startles you! You stutter out some words, "Hey…uhhh…Jesus…what are you doing here? Shouldn't you be with sheep or in heaven or with dancing angels or something? Whattt aree you doing herree, Jesusss?"

Jesus doesn't just walk into people's rooms every day. This is an atypical experience. Nonetheless, he pulls up a chair, places himself right next to you, grabs this book out of your hands, sets it on the table, looks you in the eyes, and says, "Look, I need a favor."

I kind of have a hunch of what that favor might be. I think he would ask you to start spreading the news about what he's doing in your life to other people. I don't think he would demand it or threaten you if you didn't do it. I think he would just ask politely, hoping that his love for you, clearly expressed on the cross, would compel you to do this favor for him.

Jesus might say, "Listen, I have already taken care of all your sin, and I'm working hard these days to make you the person you want to be. And you know, I want to do this for everyone. I want to help your friends, your family, your coworkers, your classmates…and some of them *really* need it. You know they do! So I'm wondering, would you refer them to me for some help? Would you just tell them that I'm willing to do this for them too? I hate watching them hurt. I love them, and I have what they need. I'll give it to them if they will just ask for it. Please just tell them…for me…will you?"

Would you ignore Jesus' request? Of course not. He's Jesus. He's kind of a big deal. Yet somehow, many of us have totally ignored the only thing Jesus asked us to do on his behalf—simply to tell other people about him. This is the mission, the only mission, he has assigned to us.

Parting Words

When Jesus was floating back to heaven 40 days after his resurrection, he left the earth by yelling down at his disciples, "You will be my witnesses in Jerusalem, and in all Judea and Samaria, and to the ends of the earth."[1]

This was the same favor. In effect, Jesus was saying, "Go tell everyone about me!"

Now, Jesus did not bring us salvation in exchange for us telling others about him. We're not saved on the basis of our willingness to tell others about Jesus, on our willingness to spread his gospel. He never said, "I'll save you *if* you become a walking billboard of the gospel."

Nope, Jesus just saved us. He did it for free, in exchange for our sin. Then he asks for one favor: "Would you just tell other people about me?" More specifically, he asks his disciples to be his witnesses.

Being Jesus' Witnesses

What did Jesus mean by *witnesses*?

Very simply, witnesses are people who verify the truthfulness of something they have seen or experienced. A witness says, "I know that John killed Bill because I saw him do it."

Jesus was saying to his disciples, "Now, please go tell people what *you've* seen and what *you've* heard!" He was saying, "You know it's true—by what you've seen, by what I've done in your own life. So go spread the news that I am who I said I am, that I can do for others what I've done for you, and that I *want* to!"

Oddly enough, immediately following Jesus' personal request for his disciples to be his witnesses, the Bible says they just stood there staring at the sky! I suppose seeing someone float up to heaven *is* a little unusual. We would probably be standing there with them, staring at the sky ourselves! Their jaws were probably on the ground.

Then, in the middle of their shock, two angels appeared right next to them and said something that was partly a question and partly a command. "Why do you stand here looking into the sky?"[2] The angels were saying, "Okay guys, get busy! You have your marching orders!"

And boy, did they get busy. Within a few years, nearly the entire Roman Empire had somehow been touched by the story of Jesus, and to this day he remains the most famous person in the world. All of this can be traced to that ragtag group of witnesses.

Christianity was more to those disciples than a personal self-help plan to better their own experience of life. It wasn't just about personally maintaining a healthy soul. Their pursuit was as external as it was internal. Their focus was not primarily on what they got out of it; it was also about what they could contribute to others and to the world. It was inside and it was outside. Christ had assigned them a mission that they took *very* seriously. The outworking of that mission in their daily activities added a new component to their spiritual lives.

Most of us isolate all things spiritual to a personal experience, and we totally avoid the mission of sharing the gospel. But by ignoring Christ's mission for us, we not only miss part of our purpose in life but also rob the world of the knowledge of Jesus. We devalue our eyewitness testimony, and we rob ourselves of the joy that bubbles out of a Christian who has had the transforming experience of personally leading someone else to healing in Jesus.

Christ's mission helps answer the ancient questions, why are we here, and what is our purpose?

The Value of the Gospel

We have all kinds of reasons for not taking our assignment from Jesus seriously.

One time, while teaching a class called Introduction to Christian Life to about 500 students, I took a survey, asking my students this question: Why don't you share your faith?

Most of them said they didn't talk about Jesus to others very often because they were afraid that they would be rejected or that they didn't know enough about God or his Word to answer the questions of inquisitive people. Some said Christians should keep quiet out of respect for other people, and others simply didn't want to, didn't care to, and didn't intend on changing their minds. In all, the survey revealed half a dozen different excuses.

I actually think all of those excuses are the result of one underlying issue. Most of us don't take Jesus' mission seriously because we simply do not value the gospel as we should. If we did value the gospel, we would willingly and regularly tell other people about what Jesus has done in our lives.

Our other excuses, such as our fear, our biblical illiteracy, or our unwillingness to engage someone in a spiritual conversation, are symptoms of this foundational problem. It's actually a simple matter. When we begin to view the gospel as we should, we will be so proud of what Jesus has done for us, our stories will bubble out in our lives and in our words. We will *want* to bring a taste of God's kingdom to planet earth, and we'll be glad to let God do it through us.

The Gospel Is the Greatest Treasure

Jesus spent plenty of time teaching about the value of the gospel. On my favorite occasion, he made his point through a parable about a couple of treasure hunters. The story is short, precise, and easy to understand. It's divided into two different scenarios spread over three verses.

> The kingdom of heaven is like a treasure hidden in a field.
> When a man found it, he hid it again, and then in his
> joy went and sold all he had and bought that field. Again,

the kingdom of heaven is like a merchant looking for fine
pearls. When he found one of great value, he went away
and sold everything he had and bought it.[3]

Jesus gives us two scenarios united by one shared action. Both men,
one a wealthy merchant looking for pearls and the other a lower- or
middle-class citizen who stumbles upon a treasure, sell everything they
have to buy one thing.

The parable shows us how we find the gospel: Some come searching for it, and others stumble upon it. But more importantly, the parable unveils for us the supreme value of the gospel. When Jesus said that
they sold everything, he meant *everything*.

The men sold their homes and their transportation, their food and
their clothing. Jesus meant to infer that these men chose total poverty
in exchange for the opportunity to possess a pearl or a hidden treasure.
They completely liquidated their assets for the opportunity to own this
hidden treasure or this priceless pearl.

The story is totally nonsensical, right? The situation is almost ridiculous! To sell everything you have to buy one thing makes no sense! How
are you going to enjoy the pearl when you have no home, no clothing,
and no food? So what is Jesus' point?

Jesus means to say that when you begin to value the gospel as you
should, you will be willing to sell *everything* you have to buy the gospel. When you begin to stare at God's gift, to recognize the glory of it,
to realize the significance of it—when you begin to be enamored by it,
to long for it—you will do anything to get it. You will be enchanted,
wooed, awestruck, shocked by it.

Later, Scripture reveals that the gospel cannot be purchased, but
can only be received as a free gift through the cross. But this doesn't
change the supreme value of it; it simply illustrates the extravagant
grace of God, who willingly distributes a gift—which happens to make
the Hope Diamond look like a rhinestone in comparison—to any pau-
per who should ask for it with the right heart.

Ridiculous, right? And so is grace!

Jesus wants his students to realize that the gospel is, truly, the most valuable gift in the universe. He wants them to really *get* what he's given them for free. He knows if they *get* it, they will begin to appreciate it.

By the way, this is also why, in the second parable, Jesus illustrates the value of the gospel by using pearls. Pearls were the most valuable commodity in the ancient world. Jews sometimes said they were "beyond price," and the greatest kings and wealthiest magnates of the Eastern world sometimes brandished their wealth by the accumulation of pearls. The primacy of the pearl is revealed in one ancient account of a competition between Cleopatra and Mark Antony. As the story goes, Antony challenged his cohort to throw a lavish party after he himself had thrown his own party. The rules of the competition were simple: Whoever was determined to have thrown the most expensive event would be declared the victor.

Marc Antony went all out. He collected the world's most sumptuous and tasteful delights and hired its most sought-after entertainers. He spent weeks and the equivalent of millions to prepare for one opulent evening, and it was such a hurrah that cleaning up the mess afterward took many more weeks.

No one imagined that Cleopatra could throw a more lavish affair, but she wasn't apt to be outdone by a man, especially *her* man. When Antony showed up for Cleopatra's version of the world's most expensive party, he was shocked to discover an uninteresting and nearly empty room. In fact, he saw only one solitary table in the center of the cavernous space with two place settings and a candelabra as the centerpiece.

Cleopatra invited her guest to take his seat just as the waiter arrived with a glass of wine, a carafe of vinegar, and a small golden box. As the legend goes, Cleopatra opened the golden box, revealing the world's largest and most expensive pearl. It was priceless.

A few aides and Antony himself watched curiously as Cleopatra retrieved the pearl from its golden cradle and dropped it in the carafe of vinegar. She sat silently until the pearl was fully dissolved by the acidic liquid. She then mixed the pearl-infused vinegar with her wine, drank it dry, and adjourned the world's most expensive party. She had handily beaten her lover, Antony, at his own challenge! He competed with his opulence; she competed with her ingenuity. Her party was *priceless*.

Of course, the story is intended to illustrate that Cleopatra was so wealthy, the world's greatest pearl was, on her whimsy, reduced to a piece of the game she was playing with her lover.

The Gospel Is Priceless and Free

Pearls, in Jesus' day, evoked a sense of mystery and extravagance. They were almost enchanting, even magical. Jesus did not choose his words flippantly. He purposely equated the gospel to the world's most valuable jewel at that time. He did this to make sure we understood what we had available to us for *free*. He hoped his analogy would stir up the same enchantment in our hearts over the gospel. He hoped we would become as awestruck by the gospel as the populace was by the pearl—so transfixed that we would be willing to sell our houses and our cars, our jewelry and our family heirlooms for a chance to be freed from sin and to enjoy a new and pure relationship with God.

Then, just as the value of the gospel is being unveiled, Jesus gives us a surprise. The gospel is not only more priceless than pearls but also available to us—for free. Therefore, we should cherish this gift. We should be abundantly grateful for receiving it, and we should appreciate the opportunity to tell this story to others.

Self-Preservation or Self-Sacrifice

We would be exaggerating and misinterpreting Jesus' parable if we claimed that Jesus presented these scenes simply to compel us to sell all our belongings to follow him. His parable has nothing to do with our material possessions; it has everything to do with the value of the gospel and our appraisal of it. If we view the gospel as we should, as it is, we will be willing to do anything for it.

I think the reason why we have such a problem nurturing this attitude toward the gospel has everything to do—once again—with our total obsession with our own self-interests. I read once that the first rule of life for most people is self-preservation, but the first rule for a Christian should be self-sacrifice.

The gospel of grace stands in stark contrast to the values of our culture, which teach us to look out for number one, to watch our own backs, and to climb the ladders of fame and fortune. The gospel makes war on our sense of entitlement, the narcissism that elevates our own interests above everything else, and our temptation to only use our leftover energy for the good of other people and for the fulfillment of God's mission. In a culture of self-preservation, the gospel calls us to be willing to do anything in order to make the world a better place. But even more than making the world a better place, the gospel calls us to put our personal effort, time, money, and every other kind of sacrifice into making the world a healed, redeemed place through the work of Jesus in and through us. The gospel calls us to self-sacrifice for its sake.

We will have the moral fortitude to do this only when we begin to value the gospel as we should.

Make no mistake about it. Scripture makes abundantly clear that Jesus has commissioned his followers to be change agents in this world. He has called us the salt of the earth because he intends for us to season the earth by our pleasant and preserving presence. He has declared that we are his ambassadors, responsible to represent the interests of the kingdom of God on planet Earth. And he has referred to us as pilgrims on an assigned mission, wandering through an earth that is not our home.

To fulfill these assignments in God's mission, we must be willing to sacrifice. The gospel always compels us to give ourselves back in its service. It doesn't require us to do it. It only requires repentance for salvation, but it motivates us as recipients of grace to be distributors of grace to a world wandering in spiritual confusion.

Singing Our Songs

Instead of exiting our churches en masse on a mission to blanket the earth with the story of God's grace, we are often focused on enjoying our relationships with God inside our churches or in our own hearts. We are apt to coop ourselves up in our communities or in private devotion while the world is crying out for what only Christ has to offer.

If we ignore our assignment to be Christ's messengers, we are guilty of robbing the world of the gift God has given them. We're like postmen who decide to steal packages instead of delivering them on our assigned routes.

God gave us grace in hope that we would also give grace on his behalf. When we deprive the world of our contribution of the grace of God, we either insulate ourselves from the world or ignore the needs of the world altogether. When we're insular, we confine our Christianity to our private, personal devotional lives, or we keep it walled up inside our churches. Eventually, we become isolated from the world around us, and we don't even know any non-Christians.

A few years ago, I stumbled upon a tragic story of a mom who had confined her three little girls to the basement of her house in Eastern Europe for more than ten years. The girls lived in squalor in a room with boarded-up windows and a single lightbulb hanging from a cord. The floor of their basement dungeon was blanketed with a thick layer of rat feces. The little girls had never learned the local language (German). Instead, they had taught themselves their own language and even written their own songs. When they were finally rescued and taken to a doctor, they cowered in the corner of the office, shielding themselves from the light because they hadn't seen the sun in more than a decade.

I think God spoke to me as I read that story. He impressed on my heart that this tragic story reflects the apathetic condition of so many Christians who are insulated from the world around them. Eventually we can no longer function effectively in the world because we have created our own world and our own hyperspiritual language. We have written our own songs and created our own culture. Of course, we don't live in squalor, but we are isolated and unaware of the world outside of our walls—a world that is desperately grasping for God through all kinds of futile pursuits.

The gospel should never be isolated behind insular church walls or the walls of our own hearts. The gospel should burst out of our walls to declare to others the testimony of Jesus from the mouths of his eyewitnesses.

The gospel is also suppressed when we intentionally ignore the spiritual and physical condition of people we know who need it. My grandpa was a country preacher who used to speak of the lostness of the world. I think that's a good image. Much of the world is spiritually and physically lost, and many people need Jesus' living water *and* a cup of cold water in his name. Yet many Christians are content to secure their ticket to heaven, receive their personal healing, and ignore Jesus' commission to take his message of salvation and healing to others.

When the church and individual Christians refuse to take their mission seriously, society can suffer incredibly dire effects. Recently, I was reading Erwin Lutzer's account of how an inactive and apathetic church contributed to the rise of Nazism. Lutzer shares an eyewitness account from a German Christian who describes the worst kind of Christian apathy. When I read it, I felt my stomach turn over.

> I lived in Germany during the Nazi Holocaust. I considered myself a Christian. We heard stories of what was happening to the Jews, but we tried to distance ourselves from it…A railroad track ran behind our small church, and each Sunday morning we could hear the whistle in the distance and then the wheels coming over the tracks. We became disturbed when we heard the cries coming from the train as it passed by. We realized that it was carrying Jews like cattle in the cars. Week after week the whistle would blow. We dreaded to hear the sound of those wheels because we knew that we would hear the cries of the Jews en route to a death camp. Their screams tormented us. We knew the time the train was coming, and when we heard the whistle blow, we began singing hymns. By the time the train came past our church, we were singing at the top of our voices. If we heard the screams, we sang more loudly and soon we heard them no more… Although years have passed, I still hear the train whistle in my sleep. God forgive me, forgive all of us who called ourselves Christians and yet did nothing to intervene.[4]

"Getting" the Gospel Means Sharing the Gospel

I guess by now someone has told you that the word *gospel* actually means "good news."

I like receiving good news, and you do too. When my wife agreed to marry me, it was good news. I told everyone I could find, I made it "Facebook official," and I raised my hands in almost ecstatic happiness. When I received my first job, or when I was invited to write this book, I erupted in spontaneous celebration. It was good news.

The gospel is not bad news, or dreadful news, or news that we should be nervous about sharing. It's good news, and it's also a message of grave importance. While we're singing our worship songs and enjoying the blessing of Christ's redemption, a whole world of people are piled on their own trains, heading toward their own kind of tragedy. We have the secret and the power to bring them liberation. Yet we often keep our good news for ourselves while they ride on to their terrible but preventable fate.

Many recipients of undeserved grace refuse to dole out grace to others. Without a doubt, this is among the greatest tragedies in history. God has assigned to us the opportunity, the responsibility, and the privilege to distribute his good news of grace to the world on his behalf.

All of us know people who need something that Jesus offers. Yet somehow we just sing louder in our churches while the world spins wildly out of control, sampling counterfeit saviors. Now is the time for Christians to go public with our faith and overtly declare our allegiance to Jesus and our belief in his power to change the world. It's time to honestly live what we believe!

Otherwise, we are lifeguards with our life vests and our life rafts and our life preservers who are content to mind our own business while the world is drowning. But Jesus is asking us for one favor: "Would you please just go help these people?"

EMPATHY FOR TERRORISTS
THE POWER OF COMPASSION

[12]

Not too long ago, I was mindlessly listening to a radio documentary on lullabies. The commentators were summarizing their global analysis of the songs mothers sang to help their children fall asleep.

I was half bored. My mind was in another place. Then the man on the radio started to talk about a lullaby sung by some of the world's poorest mothers in one of Africa's most impoverished nations. I started paying attention. The lyrics, when translated, went something like this: "If you go to sleep, hunger will go away."

It was so sad. This mother's greatest dream was that her dear child could forget her hunger for a few hours. She didn't dream that her child would one day have a house on a cul-de-sac, a nice car, a trust fund, a good spouse, beautiful children, and a secure future. She simply dreamed that her child would survive another day.

What if that was my child? What if I had *been* that child?

Let's begin with a confession. Most of us probably have a very difficult time consistently caring for other people. Despite our best intentions to help make this world a better place, despite the causes we are passionate about, the problems we know need solutions, and even a clear understanding of our responsibility to be Jesus' light to the world, we somehow struggle to consistently live the mission of Christ in our daily lives.

141

It's far easier to be like the passing priest who tries so hard to not make eye contact with the bloody and bludgeoned traveler on the side of the road. Our curiosity compels us to glance at the unfortunate plight of the beaten man lying there in the ditch, but somehow we can't get ourselves to derail our busy day in order to help someone whose problem is not our problem.

We so often ignore people who desperately need help. Every day we see people who are hurting. We live in a world fraught with relational, financial, personal, and spiritual carnage, and yet we're apt to forget by lunchtime all the pain we saw that morning in the eyes of people at work or at school. We rarely let other people's pain barge into our carefully guarded, comfortable world. Usually we are not very compassionate, and even when we are, we rarely let our compassion develop into action. We might reach a point of legitimately caring for someone, but we rarely care enough to get our own hands dirty.

Occasionally, we feel as if life has beaten us, and we hope that when we feel that way, we will receive compassion. So why can we so easily disconnect ourselves from the hurting people we stumble upon who need compassion immediately?

The Will to Fix the Problem

Compassion begins with empathy.

When we are not passionate for God's mission and not compassionate for the plight of others, the problem is usually our lack of empathy. Empathy is the ability to identify with, understand, and even feel someone else's pain or difficulty. Empathy tenderizes our hardened hearts and moves us to enter into the lives of people who are struggling through pain or difficulty.

Empathy sees a homeless person and imagines sleeping on the streets on a cold winter night. Empathy feels the emptiness of someone who searches his whole life for Jesus Christ but never has the opportunity to find him. Empathy weeps with those who are weeping and suffers with those who are suffering. Empathy softens our hard hearts.

When we choose to empathize with others, we put on their shoes, invite their feelings into our own experience, and make the uncomfortable emotional journey into their situation. Empathy picks up the tool of our imagination and uses it in compassion. It empowers us to enter into someone else's pain, problems, or trouble.

I've personally discovered that empathy is difficult to develop, but it is among the most important characteristics of people who honestly live what they believe, and it is often the spark that starts the fire of mission in believers' hearts.

Like a fire, empathy must be tenderly cared for. It must be regularly stoked. Otherwise, the fire of compassion will slowly dwindle. If it does, our hearts will begin to harden like the wax of an extinguished candle. Soon, we will once again have a hardened exterior, and we will hardly notice people who are gasping for breath.

After walking past scores of homeless people in metropolitan cities and witnessing the poverty in some of the world's most underprivileged places, after learning of the losses of friends and loved ones, after witnessing the tears of public failures and after enduring the daily montage of personal crises that arrive in my inbox, I think this remains my biggest challenge. I must become and remain sensitized to the needs of other people. If I do not, my faith will never affect the world.

Learning Empathy in the Dalai Lama's Village

On a 21-day journey through northern India, I discovered the power of empathy. Above all things, India is *religious*. It has long been called the world's museum of religions—an apropos designation. The nation throbs in religious devotion.

India boasts the historical roots of at least three of the world's twelve major religions. Nearly every road is walled up with temples, and a morning stroll down the streets of a typical city in northern India is accompanied by a chorus of bells ringing to awaken sleeping Hindu gods, the mantras of Buddhist monks, and Muslim calls to prayer. You might stumble upon Sikhs with their folksy turbans and their Gandalf beards, or you might see the fully veiled wives of Sunni Muslims. Once I ran upon a serpentine parade of finely dressed people with their elephants and camels, all celebrating the devotion of a priest who had spent his entire life in the nude.

Going to India is a trip in more ways than one.

Much of my academic work has been in religion, so India has been one of my laboratories. It was also like a second home to me during college. Mark Twain must have felt what I felt in India when he wrote that the nation "has two million gods, and worships them all" and that "in religion all other countries are paupers; India is the only millionaire."[1]

On this particular occasion, I was in the northern corner of India, where the tip of the nation collides with Nepal and China in the Himalayan mountains. Imposing snowcapped peaks glare down at the cities squeezed into the valleys. These are the world's tallest mountains, and they are as intimidating as you might imagine them to be. They make man's largest creations look like children's toys. They are the quintessential images of imposing authority.

Just on the western edge of some of these snowcapped towers rests the village of McLeod Ganj. The village teeters on the peak of a small mountain with the Himalayas on one side and a precipitous drop down into a valley on the other side. Its buildings seem nearly ready to topple over and roll down into the valley below. It appears to be perched on a pinpoint.

Being there is like visiting another planet. The city's old-world streets are always clambering with activity. The place is bursting at the seams with exotic people—exiled Tibetans, traditional Indians, and Western nomads meandering their way through the earth on spiritual quests. The Tibetan exiles are mainly monks, adorned in their burgundy robes with their shaved heads. The traditional Indian women wear their brightly colored saris and punjabis, and the Western nomads wear their tie-dyed shirts with their faint smell of a certain kind of smoked leaf.

Like the rest of India, McLeod Ganj is a multisensory place. Tibetan prayer flags flap unceasingly along the city's narrow, hilly streets. The meditating monks sing mysterious hymns that spill out of monastery windows and echo in the wind. Village lepers, forced to become professional beggars, line the streets. Most of the people living in McLeod Ganj were drawn to the city by its most famous resident, the Dalai Lama.

The Dalai Lama arrived in McLeod Ganj in 1959 at the invitation of India's first prime minister, Jawaharlal Nehru. Since that time, the

Lama's Tibetan government has operated in exile at the end of a circuitous road on the top of this mountain. Since he arrived, the city has attracted hundreds of Tibetans who narrowly escaped persecution and harrowingly fled from China by means of a 40-day journey over a snowy mountain pass.

I met all kinds of interesting people in McLeod Ganj. Perhaps the most unusual was a British woman who had, like me, travelled out of curiosity to India. She came specifically to visit the Dalai Lama. While she was there, she converted to Buddhism, decided her place was in Dalai Lama's service, and wrote her husband to inform him that they were now divorced. She has never left. When I met her, she was going on her twentieth year in the village as an ordained monk. I asked her about her progress toward enlightenment. She replied, "It's more difficult now than it was at the beginning. I think it'll take me a few more lives." Unfortunately.

When My Trip Became a Pilgrimage

So there I was on the top of a mountain in a sea of prayer flags flapping and monks meditating and lepers on my heels begging me for money. Making the journey there was a very typical thing for an overzealous twentysomething to do. I had no idea what I was doing or what awaited me. I just had a grand idea to visit the Dalai Lama's city.

I was curious. I persuaded a buddy to come with me, so we hopped a plane to India with our trusty guidebook. A few days later, after a car ride from Hades, we arrived in the Dalai Lama's village. We had no plan and no hotel—just a handful of good intentions and a hope that we would learn something and survive.

On the surface, I looked like Indiana Jones. I seemed totally confident and adventurous. But on the inside, I wondered what I had gotten myself into. On the first night of our trip, I woke up jet-lagged and burning up under India's searing summer heat. I went to the bathroom, sat on the floor, and had a minor breakdown. I could not believe I had traveled this far simply out of curiosity, and I was anxious and nervous about the whole experience. I was just glad I had brought a buddy with me. Should things go badly, at least I would have an eyewitness!

Meanwhile, God was orchestrating an encounter that would totally change my life. God really does work in strange and mysterious ways. In this case he had a lesson for me carefully disguised in a conversation with a nominal twentysomething Muslim man living in this Buddhist city. This conversation produced a drastic change in the way I viewed my life, the world, and God's mission.

Amrit

The Muslims held the rickety village of McLeod Ganj together. They operated most of the shops, many of the restaurants, and some of the hotels. India boasts the world's second-largest Muslim population, so this was not surprising. Every major city has dozens of mosques, and predawn calls to prayer frequently pierce the quiet of the night.

Muslims happen to have a lot of business savvy. Amrit was among the least faithful Muslims of McLeod Ganj, but he was one of the most entrepreneurial. He was a kind of MTV Muslim who was culturally connected to Islam but who also enjoyed dancing with the devil. He prayed hard on Friday after partying hard on Thursday, and he enjoyed the Imam's sermon as much as making love with European tourists. When I met him, I think he was about 22 and very jaded. I think that's why we immediately connected.

I had rushed into Amrit's store for a little refuge when a torrential rainstorm unexpectedly rolled over the nearby mountains. He politely invited me to dry off inside and offered me a cup of piping hot mint tea. We sat together and talked for more than an hour. Our conversation was accompanied by the sound of a monsoon swarming just outside the hanging cloth that served as a makeshift door to his roadside business.

It Makes You So Hard

At first, Amrit was very guarded. He had been well indoctrinated with a caricatured image of Americans and their caricatured opinions of Muslims, but eventually he realized I wasn't like the Americans he had heard about. I have always enjoyed speaking with Muslims and especially admire their zealous attention to hospitality. I have genuinely liked most of the Muslims I've met around the world. Perhaps that's why they have looked past their own prejudices and risked trusting me. This is what happened with Amrit. I liked him, and he started to trust me.

We drank more tea, the rain fell, and friendship sprouted. Soon he had really opened up his life to me. I learned that Amrit had grown up in the gorgeous but war-torn region of Kashmir. He told me that more than 50,000 people had been killed there in skirmishes between Muslims and Hindus, so his family moved their shop from Kashmir to McLeod Ganj. The once-lucrative tourism industry of Kashmir had been decimated by the bomb blasts and gunfights in the streets, and they hoped to rebuild their business in a new city.

I was surprised by Amrit's openness and honesty. He treated me like a lifelong friend. Eventually, with some trepidation, I felt safe to ask my new Muslim buddy a risky question. "Amrit, I've heard about bombs blowing up in Kashmir and gunfights breaking out in the streets. Have you ever personally witnessed any of this?"

Immediately, Amrit's face changed. I had triggered something in his psyche, something long suppressed and rarely revealed. The blood drained from his dark Indian skin. He wasn't angry; he was deeply, deeply distressed.

Amrit began to tell me about family members who had been killed in the violence, about childhood horrors of hearing gunshots in the streets, and about two close relatives who had died simply because they were in the wrong place at the wrong time.

Suddenly, I realized I was sitting with a civilian survivor of war. My gentle-hearted, hospitable friend had grown up in hell. His childhood was horrifying. All the pain I had personally experienced seemed so small as I listened to him, and I slowly felt myself wondering what it would have been like to have lived his life. Almost accidentally, I was embracing empathy.

The sound of the storm outside was sometimes difficult to talk over. The clouds were pelting the earth with arrows of rain, and each drop created a splash six inches tall. The scene seemed almost apocalyptic. Raising his hand and pointing at the downpour, Amrit said something that was branded onto my heart and haunts me to this day. "Johnnie, only when the rain fell like this was the blood washed off my streets."

He rolled his right hand into a fist and beat his chest just above his heart three times. "It makes you so hard, so hard...it just makes you so hard."

We finished our tea. The rain stopped. I went back to my hotel room and wept.

Empathy with Terrorism

The next day Amrit told me that he wasn't very religious anymore. He spent nearly every evening getting drunk at a local pub or sleeping with a tourist (except on Friday, when he went to the mosque). Amrit dulled his childhood pain by separating himself from God and embracing pleasure.

Later I began to think more about Amrit's decision to become a liberal Muslim. I realized that he could have just as easily gone the other way. Rather than losing his devotion to his faith after being left so emotionally mangled, he could have become a radical. Rather than running from his pain and suppressing his hurt with pleasure, his pain might have fueled a lust for revenge and a willingness to fight to the death for vengeance. Amrit could have become a terrorist just as easily as he had become a hedonist.

Islamic terrorism is often a cocktail of extremist propaganda mixed with festering, personal pain. Seasoning this mix with a touch of vengeance creates a dangerously volatile brew. This is how sensible people are persuaded to engage in a *jihad*. In a slightly different situation, Amrit might have responded to his hopelessness by becoming a suicide bomber. Life sometimes makes decisions for you, and if a few scenarios in Amrit's life had played out differently, who knows what he could have become?

My conversation with Amrit deeply affected me in a number of ways. It drew me into his experience and helped me understand and feel what life must have been like for him as a child. As we talked, empathy sprouted in my heart.

I liked Amrit. He was my age. He was intelligent. He was a hard worker who had been hurt by life and who had plenty of hang-ups but who was trying his hardest to make the best of his situation.

When he revealed to me his masked pain, I started wondering how I would have reacted had I experienced the same childhood. How would I have responded if I had repeatedly been startled out of a deep sleep by bullets ricocheting off the streets outside my home? What would I have thought about God or the world or my enemies had I attended the unnecessary funerals of people I loved?

I was somehow able to take Amrit's feelings upon my own shoulders. My imagination made a bridge from my world to his reality and sparked deep and penetrating questions. The more questions I asked myself, the more I was humbled by my own weaknesses, and the more I was burdened to help people like Amrit who had been dealt a hard lot in life.

Had I endured such suffering and horror, would I have become a hedonist, trying desperately to bury my pain with pleasure? Would I have become a hardened and angry man, haunted by bloodlust and determined to avenge the honor of my family? Who knows what could have happened? Who would I be today had I been an eyewitness of a real-life horror movie? Could I have been a murderer? Would I have had the resilience to live on with these weights on my own shoulders?

A man like Amrit may still picture his mom's or dad's blood splashed on his own clothes. He may dread sleep because he is haunted by nightmares of bombs blasting and bullets flying and his dying loved ones crying out their last screams. Millions of orphans in nations like Rwanda and Bosnia, Iraq and Cambodia, have only one memory of their parents—the day they died. Christians should care deeply for all of these people because only the grace of God allowed some of us to follow a different path. Maybe he did so for a reason—so that we could help guide people like Amrit to the Prince of Peace.

Ease Deadens Empathy, but Empathy Enlivens Compassion

Empathy is especially difficult for Americans. We live in what John Piper calls the Disneyland of the world, and we cannot imagine the suffering that some people endure. Our comfort and our wealth have lulled us to sleep. Most of us are totally unaware of many of the world's most dire problems.

Our poorest are among the world's wealthiest, and our middle class is fanatically rich compared to the upper class in many developing nations. We have a low tolerance for suffering, and we can hardly imagine the pain other people endure. Until we stop to imagine, to empathize, and to care, we will never be willing to help those who need us most. Instead, we will remain comfortable in our narcissism, we will build our own cardboard castles, and we will leave our world devoid of the contribution we could have made.

Jesus didn't save us so we could hoard all his blessings. He saved us to send us as messengers to the people of the world who desperately need him. Passion for this mission, for his mission, begins with compassion for others.

This morning I've already eaten at a busy restaurant and sat to write at a popular little coffee shop in an upscale part of my hometown. I've tried to listen to the conversations around me. I've tried to imagine the feelings attached to the words and the situations. The experience has deeply affected me.

I've listened to a couple of frustrated mothers talk about their children's misadventures. I listened to a dad yell furiously at his young child for climbing into the chair next to me, and I watched a wife lay her head on the chest of her disconnected and disinterested husband.

I've tried not to listen to people's words and watch their people behavior. Instead, I've practiced listening to their hearts. I've paused to ask myself what they might be thinking and what suffering they might be experiencing. I've tried to empathize. And I am better for it.

This experiment has activated my heart's eyes and ears. I've let my guard down and invited compassion to influence my thoughts. When compassion runs loose in my hardened interior, I suddenly feel compelled to genuinely help people. Compassion is like water to a parched and hard heart. It is medicine for the soul.

Everyone needs compassion.

In the end, I loved the city of McLeod Ganj because of the lesson it branded on my heart. It taught me empathy and compassion. I felt at home among wanderers who were searching for more in life. It was a perfect place for a missionary and for a searcher. I now realize I was both. In my searching, I found the truth that has made me a better missionary. In the ironic sovereignty of God, I learned this simple lesson from the story of a young Muslim: Empathy catalyzes compassion, and compassion empowers a person to change the world.

HOLY CALLUSES
SEEING WORK AS DIVINE

13

My wife and I enjoy evening walks. We live in a beautiful valley in Central Virginia, where the sunset turns the sky into a work of art. Man's best creative efforts haven't yet duplicated the beauty of God's ten thousand different shades of the evening sky. Often, we get a front-row seat for this exhibition. When we're especially lucky, we'll catch a glimpse of one of these displays of pure beauty during one of our evening strolls. It reminds us that God is big enough to take care of us, and we feel enveloped and small in a safe and secure kind of way. God reorients our perception of life's troubles by spreading his gigantic canvas in front of us and letting us stare in wonder. Surely, we think, if he cared enough to cast such beauty in the sky, he cares for us.

We walk just to spend a little time together. We laugh and talk about whatever is on our minds, and we admire the sights as if we were strolling through a gallery. Somehow each time we see something new. We hypothesize about who might live in certain houses, we notice when someone plants new flowers, and we keep a mental list of what ideas we might glean from the neighbors' properties as we imagine our own dream house.

I suppose we're also engaged in some form of minimal physical exercise while we're strolling through the neighborhood, but that's not our primary goal (unless I've eaten my seventeenth cupcake for the week and I'm feeling a little guilty).

Every walk usually looks the same, but on one particular evening we had an unusual interruption. We noticed a ruckus ahead of us as we rounded a corner. Kids were darting on and off the sidewalk, playing and laughing. As we approached them, a little boy who was probably four years old stood in the middle of the sidewalk, obviously blocking our path. I expected a bunch of camouflaged, mutant children to jump out of the bushes and pelt us with water balloons. I determined that if they did, I would defend the honor of my family. I would grasp each child with my titan arms and threaten to feed him to wild boars if he ever launched an attack on us again.

Kids these days are a bit more horrifying than I was when I was a little mutant. They like artists like Justin Bieber and Miley Cyrus, and they know how to hack into our computers and sabotage our digital lives. The best I could do as a naughty kid was stick my tongue out at adults I didn't like. Now, kids can steal your identity, drain your bank account on candy, and sabotage your Facebook page. They're vicious! I wasn't taking any chances!

My daydream was interrupted when the little boy in the middle of the sidewalk opened his mouth and asked in a prepubescent squeal, "Would you like to buy some lemonade?"

Thank God. There would be no assault. I answered, "Sorry, little boy, but we don't have any money."

I'm not sure he knew what money was. He looked at his little sister who was standing nearby. She said, "It's okay. Any amount of money is good, unless you're a boy, and then it's two dollars."

I tried not to be offended as I tried to determine if this little feminist was talking to my wife or if she actually thought I looked like a girl. I almost decided to go ahead and engage in the defense of my family honor and scare them till they cried, but just then, she said, "It's okay. If you're an adult boy, it's only fifty cents. It's two dollars for little boys."

So she was actually discriminating against her brother, who surely terrorized her. But I had strong suspicions she could defend herself.

Eventually, they offered the lemonade to us for free after explaining that two kinds of lemonade were available. The kids' mom made one, and the other came from the grocery store. The boy gave us a tip: "The one from the store is better."

Work Is in Your DNA

Nearly all children try their hand at being entrepreneurs. It's somehow within them, as if they were made for it. Everyone has a "lemonade stand" phase and peddles a low-cost product to as wide a market as possible with meager marketing. Most kids fail, but somehow they don't lose their will to mix more lemonade, set up more signs along the side of the road, and succeed in business.

I tried my own hand at selling lemonade once but didn't generate enough profits to buy the new game system I wanted. So I let my bankrupt business die an inglorious death and started doing magic tricks and making balloon animals. The business was far less dignified but much more lucrative. Sometimes I made enough money to buy my own lunch.

Why do we make balloon animals and set up lemonade stands? It's simple. Humans are somehow inclined to work.

I once convinced my parents to let me have a yard sale. I sold everything I no longer wanted or wanted less than a new game system. In the end, I raised more than $200. I can still remember the personal satisfaction of buying my own toy with my own money that I had earned with my own hard work. For me, making $200 was equivalent to making a million. I was rich!

This nearly universal experience is not coincidental. Almost before the dust God used to make Adam had dried, God gave Adam a job. God tasked him with tending to the garden and naming the animals. God himself is introduced to us as a worker from the first chapter of the Bible. He is imagining, building, repairing, and redeeming society, and he is always orchestrating time and history according to his intended outcome.

Both God and man have always worked. They've always been busy at something.

The New Testament also emphasizes the importance and dignity of work. The apostle Paul often spoke about man's responsibility to roll up his sleeves, dust off his tools, and get to work. He writes to a church in Greece, who was struggling with their work ethic, "If a man will not work, he shall not eat."[1] Paul amped it up even more when he wrote to his protégé, Timothy, "If anyone does not provide for his relatives, and especially for his immediate family, he has denied the faith and is worse than an unbeliever."[2]

The early church included some idle people who were very religious but also very lazy. Honestly, the situation hasn't changed all that much today. When we fail to live what we say we believe, we often simply don't work at it.

And sometimes we use our faith in God as an excuse for our inactivity. We expect God to take care of what we care about, or we expect someone else to do it, but we rarely decide to roll up our sleeves and get calluses on our hands and sweat on our brow.

Prayer *and* Work

Christians live in a tension. On one hand is God's sovereign control over the universe. On the other is Christians' responsibility to actively participate with him as he establishes his kingdom on earth.

Some Christians have an exaggerated view of God's sovereign control over creation. They assume that God has determined everything and that we're just along for the ride. On the other end of the spectrum, some Christians believe God depends completely on our work to accomplish his will. The right position is somewhere in between.

A pioneer missionary named William Carey wrote something that really helps me understand the balance between my work and God's work in the world: "We should work like everything depends upon us and pray like everything depends upon God." I think that's good advice.

Many people are deeply burdened by problems in the world or in their own lives, and they are waiting for God or someone else to do something about them. Could God be allowing us to be burdened or frustrated over something because he wants us to be change agents for the things we're so passionate and worried about?

Sometimes God allows us to be frustrated with the status quo, frustrated with some injustice, or frustrated with our situation in life. While we're waiting for someone else to do something, he is probably wondering why we're not responding to his call for us to act. Often, we are God's answer to our greatest burden, and our frustration is actually

God's way of stirring us to action. It's God saying to us, "Get to work and change this!"

Affect What You Can Control

Paul once wrote to one of his favorite churches, "Work out your salvation."[3] Paul knew that these people would never become spiritually healthy unless they decided to roll up their sleeves and start working on the parts of their lives that were displeasing to God. He was telling his friends, "You have to work at your spiritual life." He was saying, "If you want to build your faith, sometimes you have to get a hammer, some wood, and some nails, and get to renovating." The same thing is true when we observe what is broken in this world. While we're praying and praying and praying, God is looking for people who are willing to get their hands dirty. Instead, we often expect God to do all the work for us. We expect him to make the world's biggest problems disappear, just as we expect him to automatically make us into the people we want to be.

Learning to Work Again

One of the primary reasons we fail to work at God's mission is that we just don't work well at all. We are halfhearted employees, we don't work to keep our relationships healthy, we are procrastinating students…we rarely put our heart into anything unless we get big rewards in return. No wonder we don't put much effort into God's mission— we don't put very much effort into the other parts of our lives either.

All of us are inclined toward laziness at times. I tend to think my own lazy seasons don't affect anyone but me, but laziness actually often deprives the world of the contribution I could have made—the contribution God intended for me to make.

There are so many things about my life that I can't control. As much as I would like to be a finalist on *American Idol* or dance like the stars, I will always have a voice that could evacuate a burning building, and I will always have two left feet. I can't control too much about my natural talents, and creating new ones is nearly impossible. In fact, I'm realizing more and more that I can't control much of my own life story or the consequences of some of life's situations.

But I can determine how hard I am willing to work when I have the opportunity to work. Whether I'm the vice president of a Fortune 500 company or an intern shuffling papers, I ought to work hard. The apostle Paul wrote, "Whatever you do, work at it with all your heart."[4] I love what Madeleine L'Engle said: "Inspiration usually comes during work, rather than before it."

In fact, this is one of the reasons the apostle Paul was able to do so much in his life for the glory of God—he was simply a hard worker. He is perhaps the most famous missionary in history, but he was also a part-time tent maker and a well-trained scholar. He was once a determined and hardworking enemy of Christians who went from place to place seeking out those he could publicly humiliate and eventually kill. Whatever Paul did, he did with all his heart. He didn't do things halfheartedly.

Naturally, Paul worked hard for Jesus as well. After his miraculous conversion, Paul travelled to most of the populated cities of the Roman Empire on foot, on boats, and in caravans, and he endured all kinds of troubles along the way. He was jailed on multiple occasions and beaten so many times he lost count. He was stranded in the Mediterranean Sea for a full night after one shipwreck, he endured two other shipwrecks, and he was bitten by a poisonous snake. Paul knew what it was like to go without food and to shiver all night without adequate clothing or shelter in a prison cell.

Sometimes he was uncomfortable with his responsibility as a leader of baby churches, and he openly expressed a sense of inadequacy that plagued much of his life and his ministry. In fact, in one letter, Paul confessed how much of a coward he could be when he spoke face-to-face with people. He said that this is why he chose to be so confrontational in his letters. He needed to say things that he just didn't have the courage to say face-to-face. In his first letter to the church at Corinth, Paul confessed that he was a nervous and nominal speaker who desperately relied on God when he preached or taught in public. Paul may have been the kind of speaker who gets a bit sick to his stomach before standing in front of a large crowd!

Despite these limitations and personal weaknesses, Paul literally changed the world in his generation! Why? Two things separated Paul from many of his contemporaries: his determination and his work ethic.

He was willing to endure sleepless nights and repeated beatings and the shame of public scorn. In fact, he was willing to endure almost anything in order to do something he was supposed to do. Paul had calluses on his hands from making tents and scars on his back from preaching in streets. He wasn't ashamed of those scars. In fact, he proudly wore them as evidence of his commitment to Jesus, knowing that they were the price he had to pay for the progress of his mission. Despite all his challenges, Paul chose to keep working, and he put his hands and his heart into it.

On one occasion when Paul was writing about his inadequacy, he called himself the least of the apostles.[5] This was a humble statement from the man most responsible for spreading the gospel over the world during his lifetime. Then he made another remarkable statement, distinguishing him from many of Jesus' other followers: "By the grace of God I am what I am, and his grace to me was not without effect. No, I worked harder than all of [the other apostles]."[6]

Paul knew he had worked hard, and that was his satisfaction. He might not have met all of his goals, but he had done his best. He had fewer talents than some and had endured a harder road, but he had no regrets. He left it all on the field, he burned out his engines, he fought the good fight, he got back up when he was knocked down, and he ran when he didn't think he could crawl to the finish line.

Paul knew he couldn't choose his gifts and talents or control all the circumstances of his life, but he could determine how much energy he put into his mission. He chose to put all he had into all he did, and the world is better because of it. He was speaking from personal experience when he wrote, "Whether you eat or drink or whatever you do, do it all for the glory of God."[7]

Today, Paul might say, "Whether you are a vice president of a Fortune 500 company or a volunteer, your work ethic ought to be consistent. Put everything you can into everything you do, and then put in a little more."

Soft Hands and a Hard Heart

Many Christians confuse their heart with their hands. Instead of having soft hearts and hardened hands, they have soft hands and hard hearts. Rather than feeling deeply for hurting people and working hard for the good of others, they are cold to others' needs and haven't found the value of good hard work.

This is especially true in my generation. According to a major study, mine is the first generation to not include our work ethic among our top five characteristics. We've somehow lost our sense of hard work, and until we find it, we will rob the world of the contribution we were meant to make.

All of us can probably put a little more effort into all that we do. We need to mine up from our childhood the enchantment we once had for selling lemonade and mowing lawns and setting up shop. We must learn again to put a little blood, sweat, and tears into something. And we should continue developing that attitude when engaging in God's mission for our lives.

In the end, our work is not just work. It produces in our lives the incarnation of joy.

One day you'll look down and find some dirt on your hands because you accomplished something you prayed for so long that someone else would do. Can you imagine what would happen if Christians started to do what they hope others will do? Orphans would have fathers, sex slaves would be freed, the lonely would have friends, the poor would have food, and the future would be brighter for many more. Most of all, if Christians really began to work, the world would soon be redeemed. The planet would palpitate in praise of Jesus from Iran to China, from Mecca to Varanasi, and from people group to people group and continent to continent.

There are enough of us in the world to change things if we will just rise up from our indifference and choose to get into the fray.

ON STARING DOWN LIONS
FINDING JESUS WORTH YOUR LIFE AND DEATH

14

Standing where martyrs have died is sort of like experiencing your first kiss. It leaves you with an unforgettable memory that is branded somewhere onto the most impressionable part of your mind. Some call it surreal, but I think that's an inadequate description. It's more disarming. Suddenly your lackadaisical faith is shaken so violently that you almost can't bear it. Standing on the sand that was once stained with the blood of some brother or sister, you can almost hear the voices crying out again.

The Glory of the Romans

My first kiss with martyrdom was in North Africa. I entered a grand gate and walked up tiered stairs, feeling like a kid on some imaginative expedition. I was exploring an unknown world from an unknown time, and I was having the time of my life.

When I was a little boy, I wanted to be an archaeologist. I could not imagine a better life. I would get to play in the dirt all day, every day. I would explore and discover new and previously unknown secrets about the world. The inquisitive voice of the archaeologist was still alive somewhere inside me while I climbed those stairs. It posed questions and drafted theories as I stepped into the expanse of the ancient Roman structure. I was living out a dream.

The crumbling stone facade of this Roman coliseum masked its former glory, but even after 2000 years of decay, it was still intimidating. When Rome was at its apex and Christianity was in its infancy, this coliseum frequently hosted 40,000 screaming fans. It was teeming with daily activity and was the centerpiece of the entire region.

It is dead today, dusted over by time's neglect, but my imagination painted in the missing pieces as I stood inside the massive complex. I heard the gladiators' weapons crash as they engaged in their brutal games. I watched the masses erupt in laughter at comedians' antics, and I saw children sitting on their parents' laps and looking in awe at unusual and exotic species of animals parading through the arena. The building was broken and dusty and decaying, but the festive spirit still lived somewhere in the stone. The ancient walls almost have their own voices, and the long-neglected facades were straining to brag to me about what they had seen, what they had heard, and the history they had helped design.

Then I went into the mysterious underbelly of the coliseum. While the feverish crowd awaited their show, the hallways underneath the behemoth served as staging areas for the competitors and the beasts. Skylights create an unearthly feel in these long, serpentine hallways. Laserlike rays of sun slice through the black passages, revealing ten thousand dust particles. The experience was almost epic. At any moment, I expected Frodo or Aslan to pop out of some corner to take me even deeper into this fantasyland.

As I explored underneath the coliseum, I couldn't believe the intricacy of the architecture and the Romans' ingenuity. They thought of everything, and they had the resourcefulness to design and the will to build what they imagined. Fifteen hundred years before our modern era began, they lived largely like we do today. They had running water and hygienic bathhouses, saunas and spas, and beautiful buildings decorated with intricate mosaics. In fact, many Romans enjoyed a quality of life unparalleled by most of the world's population today. They were the world's geniuses and its conquerors.

Our guide was gracious as I pelted him with question after question. I asked him about the activities that took place in the coliseum, about seating for the visiting dignitaries, and about crowd control. I asked him about the stadium's size and shape and architectural design. I even asked him about the toilets! But one passing question started our little adventure down a darker path that ended with a kiss.

The Lions

Underneath the coliseum, I noticed some rectangular rooms sunken off the main walkways. The rooms were impossibly dark—nearly invisible to the unadjusted eye. In fact, I barely spotted them, and at first, I assumed they had no purpose. But the Romans had specific uses for even the smallest components of buildings, so I asked the guide what these rooms were for.

He replied, "Oh…these were the holding rooms."

What kind of answer was that? "What did they hold?"

"One set of rooms held the prisoners," he replied, "and the other set of rooms held the lions."

Suddenly the hallways seemed eerily quiet.

Then he continued. "The prisoners could hear the lions roaring as they paced back and forth in the next room. And the Romans starved the lions to guarantee a good show. So when the hungry lions caught the scent of the neighboring prisoners, they knew it was almost dinnertime. It was like a horror movie. The lions and the prisoners knew what was coming, they could hear each other, smell each other, and feel each other's presence. The prisoners could hear the lions roaring, and the lions could smell the mouth-watering meal awaiting them. They waited here in anticipation of one another. One anticipated a gruesome and imminent death, and the other anticipated dinner. The lions' stomachs growled, and the prisoners were sick with fear."

I walked inside the pitch-black room where the prisoners were held. It was cold inside. Any leftover light was swallowed up in the little cavern. It made me claustrophobic. The darkness was dense, heavy, and oppressive.

"What would someone do to deserve a punishment like this?" I asked.

"Well, they were mainly murderers and thieves," the guide said, "but sometimes they were simply Christians."

Kiss.

He continued. "As Christianity expanded, the Romans decided the Christians were a threat to their national security. They were always fearful of populist revolts threatening the stability of their empire. Christianity grew quickly, largely among the poor and disenfranchised, so the Romans felt threatened by it. All of this was aggravated by the fact that Christians frequently modified the popular chant "Caesar is lord" by declaring, "Jesus is Lord." So eventually, the Romans had enough and decided to torture, imprison, or kill some of them, hoping to squelch the movement. But their plan didn't work. The persecution strengthened the Christians' commitment, and the movement continued to grow."

The guide's brief history lesson hit me like a load of bricks. I was suddenly overcome with emotion as I realized I was standing in the very place where martyrs from another generation heard the roar of awaiting lions. If I lived then, I might have been one of them. You might have been one also, and reading this book might have been sufficient justification for your imprisonment and execution.

Nero the Horrible

The Roman emperor Nero was perhaps the worst of the early enemies of Christianity. He was an arrogant and sadistic leader who murdered his own mother, slaughtered many of his compatriots, and eventually beheaded the apostle Paul.

Nero's persecution of Christians began around the time he decided he wanted to build a house entirely out of pure gold in the center of Rome. But Nero had one major problem—no land was available in the center of Rome. If Nero wanted his gold house, he had to find a way to clear some space in the ancient world's equivalent of Manhattan.

He came up with a sinister plan. Nero secretly sent men out in the middle of the night to set parts of the city on fire to clear land for his golden palace. He paid the men and instructed them to make sure it looked like arson. Nero compensated those whose homes and businesses had been incinerated, and he had the space he needed to build his palace.

But to Nero's chagrin, the truth began to leak out into the community. People stopped believing that rogue arsonists had sparked the fires in Rome, and rumors began to proliferate in the streets that the emperor himself might have ordered the destruction of the homes and businesses.

As you might imagine, Nero was quickly thrown into a political caldron. Imagine if the president of the United States ordered parts of Washington DC to be burned so he could build himself an opulent residence! Nero had to craft a story to cover his tracks, so he decided to blame the followers of the fledging Christian movement.

Nero claimed they were the infamous arsonists of Rome, and he ordered that they be arrested, imprisoned, tortured, and executed. Some received the death penalty almost immediately. Those who didn't would have gladly traded their torture for a quick death on the chopping block. Nero was so vicious that he sometimes threw lavish nighttime parties, lighting the whole affair with the burning bodies of Christians on wooden stakes. Other Christians he dropped into boiling pots of oil, beheaded, crucified, or fed to hungry dogs. Nero might have been the most brutal and bloodthirsty early enemy of the Christian church. During his tenure, being even a halfhearted Christian was sufficient cause for imprisonment or worse.

Even more remarkable than Nero's brutality was the early believers' courage. Nearly all of them could have been exonerated if they simply denied their Christianity. In fact, many times throughout church history, Christians have been offered the opportunity to deny Christ and live. But remarkably, rarely did they choose that option. More frequently, the early believers chose death instead of denial.

This persecution continued for centuries, and its evidence is all over the streets of Europe. Early Christians were willing to die for what so few of us are willing to live for.

The Martyrs of Lyon

A few years ago, I was in the city of Lyon in Eastern France. Lyon is a typical European city with cobblestone streets walled in by old buildings with little cafés and storefronts. I remember it to be peaceful, and though it is very post-Christian, historic churches sit on nearly every street corner. The churches in Lyon feature frescoes painted by legendary artists and enormous statues of saints peering over golden altars.

But Lyon was a drastically different place in the second century.

In AD 177, Marcus Aurelius unleashed a relentless persecution against Christians in the city. First, Christians were quarantined and mocked in public baths and in the local forum. Eventually, they were herded like animals into makeshift slaughterhouses and killed while spectators watched. The victims ranged from a 15-year-old boy to a 90-year-old man, and they were often tortured near death before they were publicly and shamefully executed. Some Christians in Lyon were forced to fight unarmed against gladiators in view of thousands of cheering spectators, some were put in racks that gradually pulled their limbs from their sockets, and some were placed on red-hot iron chairs. One local deacon of a small church was beaten until he was nearly unrecognizable, and a frail female slave named Blandina was tortured over and over. Each device of torture should have killed her, but somehow she survived round after round. One historian recounts her death and the atmosphere of Lyon during the persecution:

> On the last day of the festival, the slave woman Blandina was led into the amphitheatre. After the whips, after the lions, after the red-hot plates, she was flung into a net and offered to a bull. After being tossed for a while by the animal, she no longer had any sense of what was happening thanks to her hope, the firmness of her beliefs, and her communion with Christ. For the inhabitants of second-century Lyon, Christians were part of a good day out; part of the entertainment; part of the show. The crowd—like the lions—roared.[1]

This horrific moment in history contains a miracle. Despite all the torture, all the mockery, and all the pressure to reject faith in Christ, nearly everyone who was imprisoned, tortured, and eventually murdered in Lyon and elsewhere proclaimed unashamedly, "I am

Christian."[2] If they were faced with denying Christ or imminent death, they almost exclusively chose death.

Despite being held to the fire, staring in the face of gladiators, and enduring pain beyond comprehension, these brave men and women maintained their commitment to Christ. What was it about their Christianity that made them so willing to die for what so few of us are willing to live for?

A Sense of Duty and a Fighting Spirit

The blood of Christian martyrs has long been washed from the streets of Lyon, but the testimony of that city is still alive. The streets tell the story of Christians whose faith flowed deeper than their culture and whose commitment was a matter of life or death, not opinion or fleeting feelings. Their faith was based on a conscious choice and became the foundation of their lives. The early persecuted Christians lived with a sense of duty to Christ, and their fighting spirit fueled their faith.

A conversation with a 19-year-old veteran of the war in Iraq reminded me of the common lack of duty and fight in most Christians. This Liberty University student was trying to adapt to civilian life when he vented his frustration to me.

> Duty is everything in the armed forces. But in civilian life, our generation has almost entirely lost any sense of duty to anything, even Christianity. Everything for us is superficial. We don't know how to commit to anything anymore. Instead, everything is about what's in it for us. It's like there's no nobility anymore, and there's no fight left in us.

I agree with him. Our culture seems so obsessed with preserving our quality of life that we have nearly lost values like duty and a fighting spirit.

A sense of duty characterizes people who are determined to fulfill their obligations regardless of the circumstances. A fighting spirit empowers people to struggle determinedly in opposition to someone or something that stands in the way of victory. A sense of duty led the early Christians to die for Christ rather than deny the one who died for them. Their fighting spirit gave them the courage to stare down lions in coliseums and endure the pain of persecution.

This is what Paul meant when he once wrote to Timothy, "Fight the good fight of the faith."[3] He used the language of a soldier, of war, because he knew his young friend would have to fight against a lot of opposition and distraction in order to live the life God wanted him to live. Timothy was like a Christian soldier. Soldiers are bound by duty, and they have a fighting spirit. They feel an obligation to their nation, their leaders, and their compatriots to play their role, to do their part, and to make sure that they have done everything possible to achieve victory. So they fight.

They fight when they are in pain, they fight when they don't want to, they fight when their swords are dull and their rounds are gone. They fight in exhaustion, in starvation, and even in the face of inevitable failure. They begin to lose the war only when they lose the fight that is in them.

When that young American soldier who had spent a year on the front lines of war came home, the transition to normal life in America was hard enough. But stepping into normal life in the American church was even more difficult. After fighting so tenaciously for his country's mission, he was stunned by Christians' halfhearted efforts to fulfill their mission from God.

He found that many Christians have little or no sense of duty. They don't feel any obligation to fulfill their mission, and they have little fight in them. They aren't willing to aggressively combat the sins and bad habits that are destroying them. They aren't willing to make sacrifices to take the gospel to the nations, and they don't even feel any guilt or remorse for their complacency. They don't realize they are letting down their comrades and their commander.

Many Christians have a purely personal faith that leads to an inactive, selfish Christianity. They hold rally after rally to sing and talk about their mission, but somehow, few feel obligated to actually fulfill it. Jesus is giving orders to march forward, but many Christians are in total dereliction of duty. Jesus commands an advance, but they have largely retreated. He says go, but they say no by their inactivity and their apathy. They give Jesus lip service and offer him up a tantalizing plate of good intentions, but when it really matters, they do little or nothing to complete their assigned mission.

They are AWOL.

Meanwhile, the world is bursting at its seams with spiritually sick people. Christians have orders to apply the healing gospel of Jesus Christ, but they habitually ignore their orders despite the reality that other people's lives are on the line.

My soldier friend knew that there were dire consequences for ignoring orders.

Turning Faith Outside

Sometimes we think that getting a balanced spiritual diet and tuning our hearts and minds to God's voice is sufficient for spiritual growth. These disciplines produce internal change, but they're only a part of spiritual growth. They are *means* but not the *end*. A purely internal faith is half a faith. Eventually our Christianity has to move from the inside out, and we must embrace God's mission as the mission of our lives. Regardless of our occupation or our personal ambition, we Christians are responsible to honestly and boldly live what we believe and to tell the world about Jesus Christ. It's that simple.

This mission led the martyrs of France and North Africa to consent to being killed rather than deny the gospel. This mission has also led believers through the centuries to change the world.

The early Christians felt obligated to follow Jesus when they learned of his love and sacrifice even if they had to make great personal sacrifices themselves. Once they had seen Jesus in full color, they felt compelled to live their lives for him wholeheartedly. Their commitment was logical, but it was also emotional. They felt it was their *duty* to serve the one who died for them. Jesus had sparked their repentance and sense of duty through his love and sacrifice.

So despite the possibility of imminent death, believers continued to join churches and press on to fulfill Jesus' mission. They refused to back down and deny Christ even when they faced grave persecution.

This culture of mission infused early Christianity. It galvanized the faith of the early believers and ignited the explosive expansion of Christianity in the first century.

To be a Christian in this time period wasn't easy. It required great sacrifice, yet somehow this sense of mission gave Christians the stamina to remain committed when everything in them might have compelled them to forsake their commitment.

Ironically, Christians seem to live far more faithfully when being a believer is difficult. Today, being a Christian is often easy, and in some places it's even respectable and honorable. Yet somehow we struggle to find the power to believe and to live out those beliefs. Perhaps the glaring lack of mission in the church has lulled us into spiritual sleep.

If we never embrace God's mission, we are perpetually going on first dates with Jesus. He wants so much more out of our relationship.

A Gathering of Willing Martyrs

For a while, I thought this kind of commitment was confined to ancient church history. Then I attended a commencement ceremony at a Bible school in India. The image of 2000 graduates lined up in their black gowns and hats still lives in my memory. As with our annual commencement at Liberty University, an electrifying excitement permeated the atmosphere of the ceremony. The graduates had worked hard to get to this moment, and the anticipation of receiving their degrees was palpable.

On the surface, these college graduates looked like any other graduates I had seen in their black regalia. But one drastic difference stood out in this commencement ceremony. Just before the graduates received their degrees, they stood and collectively recited a martyr's oath. I was there when they stood. In one massive movement, they rose confidently. Their heads were high, and their shoulders were back. They knew what was coming, and they had no sense of hesitation repeating these words after the president of the Bible college:

- I stand with the apostle Paul in stating that "For me to live is Christ and to die is gain."

- I take a stand to honor the Lord Jesus Christ with my hands to serve all mankind.

- I take a stand to honor the Lord Jesus Christ with my feet to spread the gospel to all the ends of the earth no matter what the cost.

- I take a stand to honor the Lord Jesus Christ with my lips by proclaiming the good news to all who hear and by edifying the body of Christ.

- I take a stand to honor the Lord Jesus Christ with my mind as I meditate upon his Word and his promises to me.

- I give my earthly treasures and all that I possess to follow the way of the cross.

- I commit to love my family, orphans, widows, lepers, the wealthy, and the poor the way that Christ loved the church.

- I surrender my will and life to his will and life.

- I commit to the service of the Lord by being a good steward of my time.

- I surrender this body on earth to the perfect will of Jesus, and should my blood be spilled, may it bring forth a mighty harvest of souls.

- I pledge allegiance to the Lamb. I will seek to honor his command. I am not ashamed of the gospel of Christ, for it is the power of God unto salvation to everyone who believes.

- Lord Jesus, thy kingdom come. Thy will be done on earth as it is in heaven.

- I love my nation and my fellow citizens, and I claim my nation for Christ.

- I have read this pledge and understood it completely. Being of sound mind and body, I do solemnly declare this martyr's pledge without any persuasion of enticement.[4]

I later learned that the man at the podium, reading the oath for recitation, had received his seventeenth death threat only a couple of days earlier. Militants had said they would shoot him while he recited the martyr's oath with the graduates. He ignored the threat. He had taken the oath himself, so he knew he was ready to die. In fact, he told me that to die while reciting the oath would be an honor.

That roar of those young voices declaring their willingness to die for Christ still challenges me. Most of the graduates that day had been raised in orphanages and trained in Christian schools, and now they were being sent as missionaries to their own people. Many of the students had fended for themselves on the streets, but in a sweep of grace, Christian missionaries had rescued them, brought them to the security of their orphanages, and cared for them in an incarnation of Christ's love.

These men and women pledged their lives to Christ because he had saved their lives. Now their greatest desire was that his message of salvation go freely throughout their nation and throughout the neighboring South Asian nations. They had decided to offer their lives in total, unconditional service to Christ because Christ had offered new life to them. They didn't require much deliberation before making such a strong commitment. It was just intuitive. Jesus' death had brought them new life, so they felt compelled to spread the news of this new life to a world desperately in need of it.

They had surrendered all other dreams and desires and were willing to accept poverty or beatings, to be robbed or abused, and to be cursed or killed if that's what their mission required. They were willing to pay whatever price was necessary to serve the one who had saved them.

A few years later, I happened to be back in India during the week that two of those graduates were martyred in the Indian state of Orissa. Thousands of Christians had fled their burning villages to live in the jungle. At the Indian church I was attending, we sang a hymn that had been written by a woman who died in the same uprising.

I knew I would soon be travelling home, where I have no concern about being physically persecuted for being a Christian. Such security might be comforting, but it's also precarious. I don't have to risk life and limb in America, but I risk a lifeless faith. I wonder how we could have the same Christ but not the same commitment to him.

Mission is the key that unlocks the door to radical commitment.

MAKING THE MIRACULOUS EVERYDAY
GOD IS AT WORK IN THE WORLD

15

W hen I was in the Dalai Lama's city, I imagined that Jesus might be at work in the village. I didn't know how God could resist the opportunity to move in a place like that one.

Nonetheless, I had almost no faith. I imagined and hoped, but I didn't expect to find much evidence of the gospel at work. I was conflicted. In some ways, I considered the city to be the most difficult place in the world for God to be at work. The village was saturated in Tibetan Buddhism, and I had never heard of a missionary even considering ministry among the Dalai Lama's disciples in northern India. Even reaching the place was tedious, and the work would be difficult and unrewarding.

When I arrived I asked God, "If you're doing anything here, would you show me?" What a weird prayer, huh?

At the end of my visit there, I struggled to veil my disappointment after seeing no evidence at all of Jesus working among the people. As I ate breakfast on my last morning, I nursed a deep, deep sadness.

My friend and I had discovered a rare American breakfast available at a backpacker's hotel. Normally, I don't enjoy eggs and bacon, but after being in India for a few days, I was relishing a taste of home. We chitchatted about the four-hour drive that would precede our train ride later in the evening. I acted happy, but I was very upset.

Just then, as absurd as it sounds, a lone traveler from Ireland who was sitting at a table next to us looked at us and said, "I think I'm going to go to church this morning."

I was shocked. It was that frank and unexpected—totally out of the blue. I said, "Excuse me?"

He said, "Oh, I think I'm going to go to church this morning. I heard there's an old British church on the edge of town. They have services in English and in Hindi in a few hours."

This launched us into an unusual conversation. The Irishman wasn't very religious, but he was very curious. He had been on a monthlong tour through India, first to visit his sister who worked for an NGO in New Delhi and then to explore the religious places of northern India. Somehow, he had reached the Dalai Lama's city and discovered a Christian church there.

I was learning from an Irish non-Christian about a church in the Dalai Lama's city. I believe this was a miracle, and it was only the first one of the day.

The "Born Again" Sermon

We went to the church. A dozen or so people were there, including the Irishman, six Dutch students on a religious tour of India, a young couple, and two older women. The pastor preached in perfect English one of the clearest presentations of the gospel of Jesus Christ I have ever heard. In fact, he spoke about the necessity of being born again. I couldn't believe it! Even in this unlikely place, God was moving by his Spirit. He led a bilingual Indian pastor from South India to the top of the world to be a missionary to his own people. He was in the backyard of the Dalai Lama's temple, faithfully proclaiming Jesus to the people in the city! It was unbelievable. I thought of David's words, "The earth is the LORD's."[1]

Afterward, the two old women sitting behind me told me they had moved to McLeod Ganj eight months earlier to pray that God would send missionaries to the city. I wondered if my curiosity to visit McLeod Ganj might have somehow been the direct result of the prayers of these women. Then I met the young couple sitting next to them. Astonishingly, they had arrived in McLeod Ganj after working for six months with a friend of mine in New Delhi at an orphanage I planned to visit later in my own trip! And one of my very good friends had been their professor at a university in Texas! God had extravagantly answered my prayer! He showed me a clear presentation of the gospel in this city, he connected me with two prayer warriors there, he introduced me to missionaries that I had some connection with, and he did it all through a "chance" encounter with a curious Irishman who had no one to talk to over breakfast!

I've discovered that when we start living what we believe, we discover that God really is at work around the world in extravagant ways, and he wants to be at work in our lives just as magnificently. If our experiences are not as invigorating as those we read about in the Bible and in church history, perhaps we have failed to live for God as we should. Christianity is only what we profess it is when we live it out the way God calls us to. When we dare to really live out what we believe, we discover that God is alive and at work on planet earth.

Jesus Is Becoming Famous all over the Globe

The gospel is moving so quickly across the earth, I'm hesitant to record its progress on paper. Today's explosive statistics of the expansion of Christianity will be outdated by the time this manuscript is published. We are living in a time when God is at work in fantastic ways all over the globe. Not since the first century has the gospel had a freer course than it's enjoying today.

Consider China. After the expulsion, imprisonment, or murder of missionaries during the Cultural Revolution, fewer than three million Christians remained in the country. Some people estimate only a few hundred thousand. Now, only 50 years later and despite the massive and aggressive movement to exterminate Christianity in parts of the country, more than 120 million Christians live in China! On one visit there, I met with an undercover missionary in my hotel. He slid a CD into my computer and opened a confidential file that revealed information on 50,000 churches that had been planted in one Chinese city! The information was so clandestine that he wouldn't let me copy it. He immediately removed the CD, but he wanted to show me the hard evidence of

God's work in that unlikely nation. By 2050, China will have the second-largest Christian population on the globe. Some missionaries estimate that every day, at least 30,000 people are baptized in the nation.

China is not an exception. Fewer than 10 million professing Christians lived on the entire African continent 100 years ago. Today, more than 360 million professing Christians live there, and African pastors are leading many of the global communions of churches. Indonesia, the nation with the world's largest Muslim population, has witnessed an incredible movement toward Christianity. At least 20 percent of the population of Indonesia professes faith in Jesus Christ. Underground house-church movements are expanding exponentially in nations like Iran, Iraq, Jordan, and Saudi Arabia. Brazil and other South American nations, which received thousands of missionaries in the previous generation, are now sending hundreds of missionaries to work among Muslims in North Africa and the Middle East.

The number one language of Christians in the world today is no longer English. It is Spanish. The average Christian is no longer a white European or American, but an Asian, African, or Latin American. The nation that plays host to the world's largest church (at least 750,000 members) and that sends the second greatest number of Christian missionaries to the world today is South Korea—a country of only 50 million people! Perhaps most astonishingly, the Bible has been translated into more languages in the past 100 years than in the previous 600 years combined. Today, some missions organizations that specialize in linguistics believe that the Bible could easily be translated into every living language in the world within the next 20 years.

Christianity may seem to be on a respirator in parts of Europe and the United States, but in actuality, it is growing and expanding in the majority of the world! Even in the United States, where Christianity is largely considered on the demise, we have seen the explosion of the megachurch movement, where sometimes tens of thousands of people gather for worship in a single congregation on a single Sunday morning. Thirty years ago, a church of 1000 people was considered exceptional. Today, some small towns have congregations of more than 1000 people. Can you imagine what would happen if the rest of America's sleeping Christians awakened to their mission to love and to serve Jesus Christ, if more American Christians began to live what they say they believe? The entire world would be shaken from its foundation by the march of the American church alone, not to mention the exponential effects of the simultaneous march of the exploding churches in Asia, Africa, and South America.

Some people are pessimistic about the potential of American Christianity. I am not. At various times in church history, pessimism has seemed reasonable, but God shattered those expectations with a surprise work of his Spirit. For example, in AD 300, the Roman emperor Diocletian ordered the burning of every Bible in the Empire. He thought that by destroying the Scriptures, he could destroy Christianity. In fact, possessing the Scriptures in certain parts of the Empire was cause for execution. But just 25 years after Diocletian's order, Rome had her first Christian emperor—Constantine. Constantine ordered the production of 50 perfect copies of the Bible—at the expense of the government!

God is at work on planet earth, and I believe he also wants to be at work in our lives. We just need to get moving forward.

The Two Things That Motivate Me

I have two primary motivations for engaging in God's work on the earth. First, I like to feel a part of something important. Second, people who have engaged in God's mission on the earth have inspired me.

When you decide to start playing your part in God's mission, when you decide to just do something for the glory of God, you immediately feel the weight of what you're doing. You're not wasting your life and your resources anymore. You feel the power of being a part of something greater than yourself, and you start to see God at work in your life as you work in others' lives on his behalf. Making a difference in people's lives is a powerfully transforming experience for you too.

As for me, I don't want to be a passing player in history. I want to make a difference in this world, and I want to leave it in better shape than I entered it. I want to live a life of significance, not of selfishness. When I meet people who've done this, they challenge me to press on in my goal.

M.A. Thomas

M.A. Thomas was a young man in 1960 when he, his wife, and a few team members decided to walk 1500 miles to bring the gospel to an infamously non-Christian city in northern India.[2] Thomas told me he had no money, a mere handful of earthly belongings, and not even a map. But he did have a sign. He had carefully written the gospel on a large placard. It fit over his shoulders and displayed the gospel on the front and the back. He decided to wear it on that 1500-mile journey so people in front of him and people behind him could have the opportunity to know Jesus Christ.

All he had was a vision that came from his deep-rooted commitment to the mission of Christ. He had taken God at his word, and he trusted that God would guide him and provide for his needs.

God did provide for his needs. In fact, a generous young missionary leader named Bill Bright discovered Thomas in South India, and he purchased train tickets for him and his team so they didn't have to walk the rest of the way to Kota, a city in northwest India. Almost as quickly as Thomas arrived, things went downhill. His gospel literature was confiscated and burned, he and his team were imprisoned, and they were threatened numerous times.

But Thomas knew God had put this burden on his heart, so he didn't give up. Soon he had started a church in the prison, leading nearly all the prisoners to faith in Jesus Christ. Eventually, the prison warden released him from the prison because he was doing more damage inside it than he had done outside! Thomas' first church was made of repentant and reformed convicts!

When I met Bishop Thomas, he had been in his city for decades, he had planted or trained church planters to plant more than 20,000 churches, he had established more than 100 schools, he was caring for 10,000 orphans, he had pioneered church planting efforts among the leper villages of India, he had received the highest possible civilian honor one could receive in India, and he had nearly been killed by radicals more times than he could remember.

Thomas was in his late sixties or early seventies when we met. He hobbled when he walked. He rocked back and forth uncomfortably on an old cane. His age had not inflicted his limbs with disease, and his joints weren't ragged from arthritis. His gait had 20 extra years on it for a different reason.

He hobbled because of the beatings he had received. Leading churches in this part of India was precarious, but he had chosen to spend his whole life there. He had suffered greatly for his decision, yet he had no regrets. In fact, his effervescent joy enveloped him. He laughed all the time—or rather, he bellowed like Santa Claus. He smiled incessantly, joked all the time, and was genuinely happy. All of this despite the trouble he had endured for the sake of the gospel. I think I first witnessed real joy when I looked in his eyes.

Despite being the archbishop of tens of thousands of churches and more than a hundred schools, Thomas chose to live in a single room just off the main entrance of his ministry headquarters. It was purposely modest. He had a bed, a chair, and a bathroom. He could have had a mansion. He chose to live simply because after a lifetime of storing up treasures in heaven, he wasn't bound any longer by the desire to have a lot of things and to look impressive to the world around him. He was obsessed with Jesus, and Jesus gave him supernatural joy in return.

One day a band of religious militants approached the front entrance of the building that housed Thomas' one-room dwelling. They were armed with sticks and a lot of anger. They were incensed that so many people were being converted and so many pastors were being trained under Bishop Thomas' leadership. They came to give him a taste of what would happen to him if he didn't stop his ministry.

Before the militants beat Bishop Thomas, he ordered them a cup of tea and attempted to share the gospel with them.

In his lifetime he ministered to millions, saved thousands of orphans, planted hundreds of churches in leper colonies, and travelled (sometimes on foot) to unreached villages in the middle of India's most difficult places. Thomas was obsessed and infatuated with the gospel, and he felt obliged to do everything in his power to reach everyone he could.

Thomas didn't challenge his mission or debate it. It was simple for him. Jesus wanted him to do it. So he did it, and he trusted that Jesus would help him. And Jesus did help him. When Thomas talked of Jesus, he seemed to be speaking of his best friend.

On one occasion, things became particularly bad for Bishop Thomas. Militants blocked the roads leading to his pastors' convention, they attacked pastors as they arrived at the local train stations, and they threw Molotov cocktails over the walls of the ministry facilities. As things heated up, the death threats started rolling in. These militants had enough of Thomas' missionary work, and they decided to put an end to it for good. So they promised to kill him if he continued with plans to celebrate the graduation of thousands of Indian missionaries the next day.

Thomas heard the threat during the convention. As soon as he heard it, he immediately hobbled authoritatively to the podium. In his booming baritone, Thomas drew his line in the sand. "There will be a service tomorrow. It will be a graduation service or a funeral service, but there will be a service!"

The graduation service proceeded without incident the next day. Thomas had called their bluff, but he wasn't trying to be tough. He simply trusted Jesus. He never thought to do anything different.

Eventually, the militants persuaded corrupt politicians to entangle Bishop Thomas in endless litigation, slowly placing a stranglehold on the ministry's bank accounts and operations. That was a few years ago, and the ministry is still recovering from years of persecution by corrupt government officials. Yet ministry leaders continue to persevere, convinced that God has assigned to them this mission.

The last time I saw Bishop Thomas, he was laying in a hospital bed. Half his body was paralyzed, and he was unable to speak. Eventually, the hard life he lived for Christ caught up with him. Some people might become angry with God, lying there paralyzed, but not Bishop Thomas. Today, he insists on a daily visit to the orphans living in one of his orphanages, he goes to his office daily, and he requires his students to read 10 to 15 chapters of the Bible to him every single day. Every Sunday he attends church, participates in communion, and becomes very frustrated if his clothes aren't carefully pressed. He wants to be at his best when he attends worship!

His son was with him at a recent church service. He gave his dad four bills in the Indian currency. He gave him three 100-rupee notes and one 500-rupee note (about $18). Thomas insisted on giving the 500-rupee note in the offering because he believed that God deserved his best.

All of us want God to do the miraculous in our lives today. We all want our own individual parting of the Red Sea to help us believe, we want to lay out our fleeces, and we tell ourselves that we'll finally sell out to God once he really proves himself to us. If he heals my disease, I will believe. If he answers my long-unanswered prayer, I will believe. I even knew one guy who asked God to move a mountain—a real mountain!

Actually, I think those are the second-rate miracles. We should pray for the much more prevalent kind of miracles that cause men like M.A. Thomas to live with a supernatural contentment despite very difficult lives. We should pray for the miracle of joy that transcends life's ups and downs, the miracle of *agape* love that gives freely despite receiving little in return, or the miracle of a new soul that has been washed clean of sin and made white as snow.

God still works in show-stopping ways. You'll see them occasionally when you finally decide to jump in. But more often, God confines his work to the place we need the greatest miracle—in our hearts.

[PART 5]

FROM MISSION TO VISION

W hat could happen if the world's Christians awakened to their potential in Jesus Christ? What if a billion Christians dared to dream big dreams and started moving forward to achieve them? What could happen if the world's followers of Jesus Christ awakened in a concert of action inspired by a deeply rooted, sacrificial commitment to Jesus Christ?

REDEEMING IMAGINATION
WHY IMAGINATION IS MEANT TO MAKE A DIFFERENCE

16

When I was in college, my little five-year-old cousin gave me a wonderful compliment. She said with total genuineness, "Johnnie, you're crazy in the head but good in the heart!"

What a nice thing for a little girl to tell to her favorite cousin! My cousin thinks I'm insane! She knew me better than I thought.

The truth is that I've always had a vivid and creative imagination. On more than one occasion, it has gotten me in trouble.

For as long as I can remember, my mind has been my little playground. I could go anywhere and do anything and escape to anyplace when things weren't going well. I could climb into the recesses of my imagination and live the life I wanted to live. I could be anyone and do anything, and I did it all the time. I burrowed my way to China and built castles out of moving boxes. I covered my toy fort in baby powder when I wanted to have a war in the winter, and I set my toy soldiers on fire when we were enduring enemy attack. I could never talk anyone into taking me fishing, so I pried the fishing rods out of our storage building and spent hours in the front yard casting and reeling, imagining each time I was pulling in the big one. I accidentally hooked myself once, but I wasn't discouraged because every true fisherman hooks himself every once in a while.

My first girlfriend was also in my imagination. We were five. She sat across from me in kindergarten. All I remember about her is her pigtails.

I never spoke to her—not once. But one day, to my mom's great surprise, when I was on the phone with my grandma, I announced to her that I had a girlfriend. I had appointed this little girl my girlfriend, totally unbeknownst to her. It didn't matter to me that she didn't know she was my girlfriend or that I had never spoken to her. I just decided that she was my girlfriend, and that was enough for me.

Once I found an old broomstick. Suddenly I was a ninja on a special mission to save the world. I most definitely was *not* a little kid with a broomstick in South Carolina. No, I was a vicious martial artist who had to defeat the enemy before the enemy destroyed all of civilization.

My arch nemesis was a tree. It wasn't even a big tree. It was one of those little trees that amateur gardeners plant when they're trying to groom their green thumb. But I had convinced myself that I was a hero and the tree was Satan incarnate. I was the protagonist. The tree was the antagonist.

I won the battle handily, and the tree died. I had saved the world! You can imagine how sorely disappointed I was when our landlord threatened to evict us if I didn't leave the trees alone. I could not believe how the crabby old lady could be so unappreciative of the fact that I had saved the world—her world!

I've been "crazy in the head" for a while.

Sometimes my imagination invited itself into my dreams. When I was in third grade, I dreamed that World War II was erupting in my backyard. So I did what any kid would do—I set up bleachers and a concession stand. I even charged admission to watch the battles unfold, and I sold refreshments to my little-kid customers.

Within the first few years of my life I was already a budding entrepreneur and the ninja who saved the world! My parents must have been very proud—or very worried.

I used my creative mind as a light saber in the never-ending wars I waged with my little sister. I made up fanciful stories about her birth and used them to make her afraid of me. She was younger but tougher, and I was always on the defensive. I didn't have brawn, so I used my overactive brains.

I once told my little sister in a tone of deathly seriousness, "I'm not going to keep this a secret any longer. You deserve to know. You're not a human! You're a robot, and if you don't start treating me better, I'm going to take out your batteries!" On another occasion I talked her into eating dog food because it was delicious and nutritious, and once I told her she was a CIA government project that we could return at any time. I threatened to put her back in her box and send her back to the laboratory. On each occasion, I delivered my case so forcefully and persuasively that she actually believed me.

I think my active imagination is what prompted me to become a magician when my parents divorced. This was another way I could escape from my difficult world. Nearly every day after school, I ran to my room and to a deck of playing cards. I stayed there for hours fiddling around with magic tricks. Before long, I was helping support my family by doing magic tricks at a little restaurant in town, and eventually, I won second place at a national sleight-of-hand competition.

I now know that my desire to be a magician had a little something to do with my desire to make the world a better place. I wanted to live in a world seasoned with miracles because the challenges facing my family could be solved only by the miraculous.

The part of me that longed for God's help was the same part that longed for these little counterfeit miracles. From almost the beginning, something within me has cried out for the miraculous. I have always believed that this material world includes more than meets the eye and that the impossible could be challenged and overcome.

Fighting to Preserve My Imagination

As I've gotten older, my imagination has become less active. Life has a way of waking you up. It forces you to trade in your illusions of grandeur for a hard, cynical realism. When you're a child, your imagination is colorful as a rainbow. When you become an adult, it takes everything in you to keep your imagination from fading into black and white.

Those special people who can preserve their imagination become artists, and most artists will live financially impoverished and socially unappreciated lives. A few of them will be fantastically rich. Either way, people who live for art have refused to let their imagination die.

In a sense, they haven't grown up. Living this way is not a mainstream, adult thing to do. People think critically and cynically about artists who seem perpetually confined to their imagination. Yet despite all the jokes about starving artists and the paintings of abstract artists, many of the world's greatest connoisseurs of fine art are among the most stoic and sophisticated ones of us. Could such stoicism be a glossing over of an internal search to find again one's long-lost imagination?

We're taught to put away our imagination, get a career, join the daily grind, and work to put *that* car in your driveway at your house in a cul-de-sac so that your 2.5 kids will grow up to do it all over again. Nine-to-five becomes the rhythm of life, and we forget how to play. We only know how to check things off a task list and press on through the scheduled and structured reality of adult life. Eventually our imagination atrophies, and soon it's harder to laugh and to cry. Life moves on without much *life* in it anymore.

God Created Imagination

Everything God created seems to have a purpose, right? Could it be that God's creation of imagination wasn't just for our childhood, but for our whole life? Maybe God doesn't want our imagination to die to the cynical realism of everyday life.

After all, if God created it, we ought to ask ourselves, what is its purpose? He imagined imagination for a reason. In fact, God wired our imagination into the most complicated part of our human machine. Imagination lives somewhere in our three-pound brains. We've seen that the brain contains 100 billion interconnected neurons making 100 trillion connections between themselves. Each of those 100 trillion connections is capable of performing 200 calculations per second. The human mind remains as much of a final frontier to scientists as do the outskirts of the universe.

An information scientist helped me appreciate the majesty and the complexity of the human brain by comparing it to the Internet. In an online lecture, he said that in 2007, the entire World Wide Web contained 55 trillion links; it processed 2 million e-mails per second, 1 million IM messages per second, and 100 billion clicks a day; and it used up 5 percent of the globe's electricity. Stunningly, the Web processed 7 terabytes of traffic per second, which meant that every three seconds, more data traveled through the Internet than is contained in the entire Library of Congress.

Then the lecturer said something that totally floored me. "The entire World Wide Web in the year 2007 was roughly equivalent in complexity to one human brain."

Wow. Our imagination lives somewhere in this vast and complicated creation of God. Somehow, I don't think I'm getting full use out of my mind and my imagination!

When I heard this lecture, I reacted in two ways. First, I stared at the guy on my computer screen for a few moments with a flabbergasted look on my face. I was probably drooling in awe. Second, I asked myself why God installed such an incredibly complex and creative machine inside of us. Surely there's more to this than playing games, painting paintings, and writing books. I wondered why God invested so much in our minds and in our imagination. What role are these meant to have in our lives?

I think our imagination is the part of the image of God inside of us that reflects God's creativity. Our imagination is a distant cousin to what caused God to think of Mount Everest and the Grand Canyon, the warmth of true love and the grandeur of a seemingly endless universe. Our human imagination is a highly diluted version of what inspired God to dump immeasurable gallons of water into our oceans and to pivot earth on just the right axis to bring us life. It's what caused God to think of a barrier reef, make leaves change colors, and think of making bees with stingers the source of sweet honey.

Have you ever tried to imagine something from nothing? Have you ever tried to envision a totally new animal, tree, planet, or place? It's almost impossible to not slide into science fiction. The fact that God could draw up such a complicated and interwoven universe is simply beyond comprehension. Yet in our imaginations, God seems to have deposited a bit of that characteristic in us.

Perhaps God gave us creativity for a purpose. Clearly, God went to great ends to allow us to see beauty and to contemplate different realities, to play with imaginary friends and to write poetry, to direct movies and paint landscapes and write love letters. But maybe God's purpose for creating our imagination transcends all of that. Maybe it's more than simply a vehicle for entertainment.

Our imagination wasn't a halfhearted afterthought in God's creation of man. It wasn't meant to just make us laugh or cry in a great movie or to give us relief in a particularly stressful season of life. It must be more than a device for creativity and for helping children escape from their world and enter into another.

Maybe God gave us this mind and imagination as an investment of his own creativity into our potential, and maybe God means for us to use our imagination to see our lives and our world differently.

Imagination Is the First Step to Vision

When we start to engage our imagination in a pursuit of God's mission, we become visionaries. Vision begins with imagination.

A lot of Christians I've met throw around the word *vision* a great deal. They use it as if everyone knows what it means, but I'm not sure everyone knows what it means to have vision. So let's define it.

Of course, I'm not speaking of physical vision. It's not the vision that enables me to see to type these words or that these contact lenses correct in my eyes. I'm speaking about vision as the characteristic of certain people who see the world and their lives in a way that is different from what it actually is. Some people sometimes use the word *vision* as a synonym for *dream*. When Martin Luther King Jr. trumpeted from the Lincoln Memorial, "I have a dream," he was referring to a vision. It just wasn't quite as poetic to say, "I have a vision!"

Having a vision is actually more than simply having a dream because vision implies a certain degree of assuredness, of faith. People with vision not only see what could be but also start to believe that one day, what *could* be *will* be. Vision is a means of actualizing faith. It is the ability to somehow know that your dream will happen—perhaps in your lifetime, perhaps in another. It is a quintessential act of living what you believe.

Through the centuries, vision has been a vital part of the Christian church. It is the characteristic that inspired the people of God to continue marching forward despite great opposition. It caused Israel's leaders to see the promised land from within the desert. It was vision that enabled Nehemiah to see a rebuilt wall around a conquered and crumbling Jerusalem, and vision that spurred the early church to march their faith toward Rome. It was vision that empowered the early Christians to believe that despite their prison cells, persecution, and martyrdom, the gospel would one day cover the earth. It was a vision of reform that caused Martin Luther to spark the Reformation with his 95 theses, that caused Martin Luther King Jr. to see a day of desegregation, and that gave Winston Churchill the strength to believe that justice would reign over hatred in the Second Great War.

Vision is the enemy of hopelessness and doubt. It is the enemy of the status quo, of pessimism, and of stagnation. Vision stirs the stale water of settled reality into things new and once unimaginable. Vision presses us on to better places, girds us up when our imagined goals suddenly seem possible, and builds scaffolding around weakened faith during seasons of doubt, trial, and frustration.

Vision sees the world as different than it is today.

King Solomon knew this when he declared, "Where there is no vision the people perish."[1] The writer of Hebrews had vision in mind when he said, "Without faith it is impossible to please God."[2]

Vision Is the First Step to Transformation

Christians are not content to remain where they are. Christians move forward, they progress, they are always being transformed, and they are always working to transform the world. Christians don't see the world as it is. They see the world as it might be and as it could be if God rained down his grace in response to their prayers and their labor.

Vision is also the faith to see your own life in a different place than it is today. It is the ability to anticipate the day your soul will be healthy, your family will be restored, or your life will feel alive again—the day when things will be different.

And if imagination is the source of vision and vision is our time machine to see what will be, then vision is the tool to pull us out of the dredges of the mundane and plant our feet squarely into the prospect of hope, of what could be. There are no limitations to our imagination, and there should be few limitations to vision. We can see a world with no war and no poverty, a world where benevolence is more attractive than revenge. We can see a different reality for ourselves and for our future. We can see the gospel bursting forth in brilliant radiance in the most barren places of an irreligious world. We can see our dead churches coming alive and our apathy turning into passion. We can see our divorces in reconciliation, our children in submission to God, and our marriages saturated in joy. Our wildest dreams suddenly seem to be tangibly real.

Imagination becomes vision when our dreams reflect God's will for our lives.

What do you wish was different in your life and in the world? What is God's will in that situation? Use your imagination to see it and then ask God for the faith to believe that what you're imagining is coming. Ask God if he desires for you to be one of the tools he can use to make your vision of his will a reality.

One of my mentors used to frequently challenge people with a simple but profoundly powerful question: What would you do if you *knew* you would not fail?

What would *you* do if you knew you wouldn't fail? Maybe now's the time to harness your imagination and start envisioning what could be.

BECOMING DOMINOES
HISTORY'S CASTING CALL

I know. Like me, you feel pretty insignificant sometimes.

You get up in the morning and go through your day, return from school or work, eat something, watch some TV or surf the Web, and go back to bed for another night of dreamless sleep. Or if you dream, you're always the victim and never the hero. Then you do it again and again, day after day, like a lab rat sleeping, eating, and bumping into the same walls in the same way time and time again. Most of us live predictable lives, as if we're in a recording on replay.

Life *can* get pretty mundane and repetitive sometimes. Sometimes life bores you to death, and sometimes it beats you up. Life can be like one of those bullies with no neck and no brains that bludgeons you for the fun of it, or it can be a slow grind that wears you away moment by moment, day by day. When life is vicious, it doesn't kill you quickly. No, it tortures you slowly, painfully. It's like watching *High School Musical* with your 12-year-old cousin *again*.

With too much of this treatment, you can begin to feel insignificant and dissatisfied with even the great things in your world. Dissatisfaction is actually a message screaming at us from the recesses of our soul. Our soul is begging us to turn away from what we think is important and focus on what really *is* important. The remedy for our dissatisfaction is paying attention to our soul and to God's desire for our lives, and to live for the glory of God and the good of man.

Sadly, most of the time we misinterpret the dissatisfaction, and we embrace an insufficient remedy. We start grasping for anything that injects a sense of fulfillment or change in the rhythm of our mundane routine. We'll do almost anything to dress up our boring story. We think that the dissatisfaction is simply boredom, and the remedy for boredom is change. So we move to another city or quit our job or change our major or enroll again in school or drop out of school or break up with our girlfriend or call an old friend or try a new hobby or go to New York or backpack through Europe. We might throw away all our material possessions, grow some dreadlocks, and become nomads. (This, by the way, is the first step to becoming crazy. Eventually, you'll be sitting on the porch of your mountain shack, looking at your yard full of cats and wondering when a spaceship is coming to take you to Narnia to meet Yoda.)

Discontentment can lead us to strange places.

When we don't like our lives, when we're discontent, we think that all we need is a change, and almost any change will do. So we change for the sake of change, somehow thinking that injecting a little unfamiliarity in the mundane will make life glorious.

It works temporarily. Change for the sake of change makes you feel excited again about the everyday. Change can be like salt and pepper on bland food. Change for the sake of change becomes a temporary antidote for a dissatisfying life, and it is temporarily satisfying.

It's not that change is bad. Some change is good. In fact, much of this book is about the right kind of change. It's just that much of the change we make in our lives is inadequate. We need truly transformative change. Otherwise, we're putting those cartooned-painted children's Band-Aids on our gushing wounds. Change becomes a temporary relief for more permanent and unaddressed problems—problems that will fight to get your attention until they find resolution.

Eventually, after enough change for the sake of change or enough difficult seasons in life, we begin asking ourselves deep and difficult questions about the meaning of life. Why am I here? Is there more to life than this?

I've been there. I asked those questions when my parents divorced, our house went into foreclosure, and my dad tried suicide. When everything seems broken and too many problems pile up in too short of a time, you probably also ask those hard questions too. Soon crisis of belief follows crisis of belief, and the values and beliefs you once held so tightly become negotiable and questionable. The few things that were once unquestioned in your life are put on the table, and all of a sudden you start feeling as if the foundation of your life is no longer solid. You feel insecure and disillusioned.

For some reason, we tend to respond to these seasons by blaming God rather than running to him. The only one we really need becomes the only one we can find to blame when we have too much pride to blame ourselves. I've been there too, wandering through a maze of confusion about life and faith.

At first, you think these seasons and questions are dangerous. They cause you to doubt and to become increasingly dissatisfied with the status quo. They are enemies to your settled beliefs, and they make you uneasy and anxious and sometimes even angry at life, at *your* life. But actually, these are the questions you must ask yourself if you're ever going to stand out from the pack and become the person you dream about being, the person God designed you to be.

Only after asking the difficult questions will you believe the answers that you discover, and only after enough dissatisfaction with the way the world is, the way *your* world is, will you find the motivation to work to make it a different place. Only then will you embrace the right change, one that not only changes your perspective on life but also makes you a change agent for others who are wandering aimlessly through their minor-league misery on their own personal mission to discover why *they* are alive.

I now know that these seasons of my life weren't actually crises. They were the moments through which I came into my own belief, and I started getting honest about living what I said I believed. I was beginning to own what I had inherited from my Christian culture and my parents' church. I was becoming my own kind of Christian. Without those moments, I probably would have continued to live off the fumes of my family's fragile and failing faith. My affinity to skepticism would have been fueled by the hypocrisy I observed in the church and in the lives of the Christians I knew the best. I would have ended up hopelessly self-deceived.

Eventually, I would have lost my love for Jesus and my commitment to his mission. I might have still proudly adorned the Christian label, but it would have been more about my culture than anything else. I wouldn't have been living honestly. Many of the Christians I know will live their whole lives this way. Their commitment to Jesus will be a matter of culture or politics or family but not of honestly living out their beliefs. They will miss it all.

The anxiety of dissatisfaction and the ashes of failing faith can somehow lead to the greatest, most committed belief. The struggle to own your belief can reveal the power of your faith. After a few battles, you may realize that your faith is the only settled thing in your life and that it is worth fighting for. Eventually, you start to live what you really believe, and you exchange your cultural Christianity for the kind of living faith that shakes the mountains and parts the seas and makes lions lay down with lambs.

I wrote this book because I wanted to help you get there. I wanted to help you crawl out of the mire of Christian culture, to discover real faith, and to begin to see your world through fresh eyes. I don't want you to be one of those Christians who fade in and out of their scene, nearly unnoticed, and I especially don't want you to live your life with a form of godliness but no power.[1] I want you to have a living, breathing, experiential faith.

Actually, this isn't much of a book. It is more of a personal confession, a plea, and an invitation. It's an honest confession—not from a teacher, but from a fellow student who is on a journey of his own—that addresses some of the things we're afraid to talk about. It is a plea to wake up out of sleepy faith and into new vision. And it is an invitation for you to embrace a new way of thinking about your life and your world.

All of it has come from somewhere in the deep recesses of my heart, where I want to cry out to the generation of men and women living today to embrace their greatest potential for the glory of God. It is a plea to the old and the young to live what they believe with abandon and without reservation or qualification.

In my imagination, I see men and women becoming what they

could become if they chose to believe and to live. In fact, I can see you there in my imagination. You are stepping into your own, out of the background and out of the pack. You're standing your ground, claiming your space, and making your mark. I can see you there. I hope you can see yourself there.

It's a beautiful vision.

It's a vision of a world where Christ is known because of his followers, not in spite of them. It's a world where all believers take their faith seriously and enjoy the opportunity to affect their world for God's glory. It's a world where more than a billion Christians come alive and choose to invest their resources, their time, and their potential to press on in the mission of God.

It's a world where the compassion of Jesus causes his followers to help eliminate poverty and injustice, to reach the unreached, and to awaken the world to its Redeemer.

A Closing Word

I believe that as an actor in history's play, you are more important than you think you are. I have a hunch that history's best stories have not yet been unveiled and that you have an important role in some of those stories.

Minute by minute, your life may seem to move along at a lethargic pace and to be filled with insignificant activities. But all the parts and pieces form acts and scenes in one enormous and interconnected story that God is producing. Your part in God's story is meant to make this world a better place, and it's important.

May I just ask you this? Please play your part, and play it with abandon. Each of us, as we awaken to living belief, can do a little more to make things a little different. Please, don't live as a spectator. You're not one of the extras in the background of an exciting scene that someone else is enjoying. You are a supporting actor in something wonderful, a story worth telling, a story that could affect the future of millions upon millions of people.

When I was a child, I was infatuated with dominoes. The dominoes were pieces of a game, I guess, but I never knew the rules. I was content to set them up and let them tumble again and again. I carefully arranged those little black and white pieces of plastic in a long and curvy line. Situating the dominoes in the right way seemed to take forever.

Then, with my index finger, I barely touched the first domino—just hard enough so it would teeter and finally fall. Then I stepped back and watched in awe at the exponential effect of that one action. In seconds, that single action triggered each successive domino to fall, one after another, all the way to the end of the line.

I was fascinated by the effect of that one little action. I am still fascinated by the potential effect of little actions. Who knows where a conversation will lead, what one act of compassion will spark, what one encouraging word will do, and what one person whom I introduce to Christ might accomplish?

Domino moments happen all around us. Moments where seemingly insignificant acts, brief conversations, or chance encounters trigger a few things that trigger many other things. Before you know it, something wonderful is happening. These are the domino moments.

We all are dominoes in God's story. And eventually, we might find ourselves to be unlikely leads in unlikely stories that change the world as we know it. What if you're the missing piece in some fantastic story waiting to be told? Maybe the next big story is yours to improvise. Maybe the next move is yours to make. Maybe you're the domino God will use to do something unprecedented in all of history. Maybe this book is a domino. Maybe this moment is a domino moment that could change everything.

This book asks, what if...? What if you had the initiative to throw yourself into the fray, to imagine and to dream, to work and to pray, to serve and to live a radical life fueled by radical belief? There are challenges to be triumphed, diseases to be cured, lives to be saved, causes to be embraced, people groups to be reached, and ten million problems that might be opportunities to redefine the world.

Every once in a while someone walks onto the pages of history with just enough discontent with the status quo to change things for real. What if you are one of those people? We have to live as if we are. Otherwise, we might miss our moment, and the world might miss our contribution.

A man named Henry Varley inspired D.L. Moody by saying, "The world has yet to see what God can do with one man fully consecrated to him."

Moody replied, "By God's help, I aim to be that man."[2]

I have been writing in the spirit of those comments. When I read Moody's reply, something inside of me jumps to attention. I too want to be that man. I don't want to quiet that voice in my heart any longer. I want to listen to it, and I want to live it. Will you join me? Or will you go unnoticed?

What could happen if a billion Christians came alive? Will you be one?

I dare you. I dare you to be more for Christ, to believe more deeply, to live that belief with a stronger commitment, and to flick a domino or two on the chance that the world is waiting for it.

AFTERWORD

Once I saw a neglected, unfinished house in a gorgeous neighborhood.

Every other house was like a fortress. No doubt, each one was the culmination of someone's lifelong dream. All of them were customized to the hilt, trimmed with imported woods and marble, guarded by a gate, and adorned with at least one brand-new luxury car in the driveway. The walkways leading to their towering front doors were inlaid with customized mosaics. A sense of extravagance emanated from the homes as I drove through the neighborhood.

Then, in the middle of luxury, sat this oddly unfinished and clearly neglected home. It was the ugly duckling of the neighborhood. It was an eyesore in the middle of architectural masterpieces. I imagine the owners of that home had a good reason not to finish it. They must have run out of money, or their marriage fell apart, or maybe they had just lost the will to finish what they had begun.

Our spiritual lives can be like that neglected house. Sometimes we don't know how to overcome our unfinished struggles, and sometimes we just lose momentum. We don't live what we believe.

I hope that through this journey, I have given you the tools you need to finish what is unfinished. Even more, I hope you've found the will to turn your attention to what you might have neglected. But all the advice and all the encouragement in the world can't make you change what needs to change. Eventually, you just have to do what you know you need to do. There's always a next step. Your next step probably fits squarely within one of the five sections of this book. You might need to get answers to some of your questions, or work to get a more balanced spiritual diet, or to learn to trust God even when you can hardly see him, or get engaged in God's mission, or find a greater and bigger vision for your life. Or maybe it's a little bit of each.

By reading this book, you have taken another step in your journey. It's not the end-all. Please take that next step toward living what you say you believe. If you do, the next time we meet, we'll both be different people.

NOTES

Chapter 2: Proudly Doubting Thomas

1. John 20:25.
2. Benedict Vadakkekara, *Origin of Christianity in India* (Delhi, India: Media House Delhi, 2007), 131.

Chapter 3: The Liberation of Belief

1. Elie Wiesel, *Belief* (New York, NY: HarperOne, 2010), 160.
2. John E. Hare, *Oxford Studies in Theological Ethics: The Moral God, Kantian Ethics, Human Limits and God's Assistance* (Oxford: Oxford University Press, 1996), 93.

Chapter 4: Belief in the Ashes of Genocide

1. Hare, *Oxford Studies in Theological Ethics*, 135.
2. Ibid.
3. John Rucyahana, *The Bishop of Rwanda* (Nashville, TN: Nelson, 2007), xv-xvi.

Chapter 5: We Are All Orphans

1. 2 Corinthians 8:9.
2. 1 Corinthians 6:20.
3. Ephesians 1:4-5.
4. Romans 2:4.

Chapter 6: The Necessity of Soul Food

1. Doug Groothuis has addressed the misunderstanding that this is a quote of Blaise Pascal. See his blog entry at theconstructivecurmudgeon.blogspot.com/2006/05/incorrect-pascal-quotes.html.

Chapter 7: Tuning Your Ears to the Voice of God

1. Brad Young, *Meet the Rabbis* (Peabody, MA: Hendrickson, 2007), 155.

Chapter 8: Giving In to the Will of God

1. Exodus 20:3.

Chapter 9: We Are "Get Back Up Again" People

1. Romans 8:37.
2. 2 Corinthians 4:8-9.
3. Hebrews 12:12 ESV.
4. Psalm 91:7-11.
5. Matthew 5:45.

Chapter 10: When Your Ship Wrecks

1. Frank J. Metcalf, *American Writers and Compilers of Sacred Music* (New York, NY: Abingdon, 1925), 304.
2. 1 Peter 5:7.
3. Job 42:5.
4. Philip Yancey, *Prayer* (Grand Rapids, MI: Zondervan, 2006), 136-37.
5. Cited in Yancey, *Prayer*, 137.
6. William Lane Craig, *On Guard* (Colorado Springs: Cook, 2010), 158.
7. Isaiah 55:9; Romans 8:28.
8. 2 Peter 1:3.
9. 1 Corinthians 15.
10. Romans 10:9.
11. 2 Corinthians 1:9.
12. For more information on this, read chapter 7 in Mark Driscoll's book *Vintage Jesus* (Wheaton, IL: Crossway, 2008) or read any of the writings of my colleague and friend Gary Habermas.
13. 1 Corinthians 15:54-55.
14. 2 Peter 1:30.

Chapter 11: Going Public

1. Acts 1:8.
2. Acts 1:10-11.
3. Matthew 13:44-46.
4. Erwin Lutzer, *When a Nation Forgets God* (Wheaton, IL: Moody, 2010). Cited in James Robison, "Will the Church Just Sing Louder?" www.jamesrobison.net/?q=node/42.

Chapter 12: Empathy for Terrorists

1. Mark Twain, *Following the Equator* (New York, NY: Harper and Brothers, 1899), 72.

Chapter 13: Holy Calluses

1. 2 Thessalonians 3:10.
2. 1 Timothy 5:8.
3. Philippians 2:12.

4. Colossians 3:23.
5. 1 Corinthians 15:9.
6. 1 Corinthians 15:10.
7. 1 Corinthians 10:31.

Chapter 14: On Staring Down Lions

1. Christopher Kelly, *The Roman Empire: A Very Short Introduction* (New York, NY: Oxford University Press, 2006), 78.

2. See Joseph Ernest Renan, "The Martyrs of Lyons," in *History of the Origins of Christianity: Book VII—Marcus Aurelius.* Available online at www.ccel.org/ccel/renan/marcus.xxii.html.

3. 1 Timothy 6:12.

4. Hopegivers International, "Martyr's Oath." www.hopegivers.org/What-We-Do/Martyrs-Oath.htm.

Chapter 15: Making the Miraculous Everyday

1. Psalm 24:1.

2. Archbishop Thomas passed away in India in December, 2010.

Chapter 16: Redeeming Imagination

1. Proverbs 29:18 KJV.

2. Hebrews 11:6.

Chapter 17: Becoming Dominoes

1. 2 Timothy 3:5.

2. Henry Blackaby, *Experiencing God* (Nashville, TN: B&H, 2008), 47.

ABOUT THE AUTHOR

Johnnie Moore is a twentysomething Christian who serves Liberty University—the world's largest Christian university and the seventh-largest university in North America—as a vice president, the campus pastor, and a professor of religion. He is best known as a popular speaker in the university's campus services, North America's largest weekly gatherings of Christian young people. He has traveled to more than 20 nations on missionary and humanitarian excursions with Liberty University students, he is a member of the board of trustees of World Help, and he serves as a communications advisor to educators, preachers, and politicians. He and his wife, Andrea, live in Lynchburg, Virginia.

www.johnniemoore.org

www.liberty.edu

www.worldhelp.net